D1738521

PARADOX OF CHANGE

PARADOX OF CHANGE

The Rise and Fall of Solidarity in the New Poland

William Dan Perdue

Westport, Connecticut
London

Library of Congress Cataloging-in-Publication Data

Perdue, William D.
    Paradox of change : the rise and fall of Solidarity in the new
Poland / William Dan Perdue.
        p.   cm.
    Includes bibliographical references (p.   ) and index.
    ISBN 0–275–95295–9 (alk. paper)
    1. Poland—Social conditions—1980- 2. Poland—Politics and
government—1989- 3. NSZZ "Solidarnosć" (Labor organization)—
History. 4. Post-communism—Poland. I. Title.
HN537.5.P455 1995
306'.09438—dc20   95–7551

British Library Cataloguing in Publication Data is available.

Library of Congress Catalog Card Number: 95–7551
ISBN: 0–275–95295–9

First published in 1995

Praeger Publishers, 88 Post Road West, Westport, CT 06881
An imprint of Greenwood Publishing Group, Inc.

Printed in the United States of America

The paper used in this book complies with the
Permanent Paper Standard issued by the National
Information Standards Organization (Z39.48–1984).

10 9 8 7 6 5 4 3 2 1

Contents

Preface

The ongoing struggle in the New Poland is not confined to the daunting questions of economic transformation, though these have certainly seized center stage. Troubling the dreams of Polish democracy is the more recent splintering of *Solidarnosc*, the party, and its estrangement from Lech Walesa, the man who led it to institutional power. Complicating the abstracted idealism of political liberty is the difficult construction of grassroots democracy, hampered further by the lingering political culture of an authoritarian order. Cracking the solid wall of Polish Catholicism are more secular missions, one past and one present. The first was to give spiritual sustenance to the liberation forces of the eighties. The second is to seek wider institutional influence in the last decade of the century. It is almost trite to say that Poland faces a new legitimation crisis at the political level. There is instead a higher turning point, which leads a sociologist and colleague in Krakow to worry about a Durkheimian collapse of normative and moral authority across institutions.

In historical retrospect, one thing is certain. The bipolarity of the cold war era created an ideological dichotomy (in Poland as throughout East and West). The result was to deny rival conceptions of development and institution building. Before the collapse of the U.S.S.R., the world was simply divided into market and command economies. The systemic intersection of these idealized types in the world market was often overlooked, as superpower rivalry took the form of a modern morality play of good and evil. Weighted down by a system in which often corrupt political decisions drove the productive life of a society, by the omnipresent threat of tyranny, by the absence of viable and authentic institutions of civil society, by the waste of state militarism, and by technological isolation and world market disadvantage, the U.S.S.R. and its proxy states in Eastern Europe finally collapsed. In the aftermath, those who had embraced the absolutism of bipolarity rushed to declare a new dogma: that of unipolarity. Francis Fukuyama declared the end of history and the triumph of "liberal democracy." However, history has a way of moving beyond ideology.

It is true that idealized and reified conceptions of "real socialism" under the Soviet system camouflaged promises unkept in Poland. It is also true that empty rituals on the part of the party-state led to a succession of legitimation crises. However, the rise and triumph of Solidarity was driven by something higher than the collapse of party-state authority. In the pages that follow, the reader will find that above and beyond the legitimation crisis in Poland loomed a higher and multilayered systemic crisis. The attempts of the U.S.S.R. and the party-states of Eastern Europe to build collective self-sufficiency through COMECON (Council for Mutual Economic Assistance) had clearly failed by the mid-1980s. This denouement cannot be seen in isolation. From the 1970s, the states of the second world had increasingly sought to finance growth and development through debt and trade. Political advocates and controllers of centralized command economics wagered they could play the world market game. They also failed. These were not simply problems of party-state tyranny and incompetence, though these were real enough. It was instead that the classical dependency relation had emerged--not simply between the U.S.S.R. and its satellites--but between East and West. Today, the shattering of the former relation does not guarantee the negation of the latter.

As a new century now gives evidence of the pangs of birth, this is a time of promise and peril. What has been described in some circles as the Polish transition misses the profound institutional crisis and the higher milieu of conflict and change. This is not a mere passing from one side to the other through the acquisition of technical skills--it is a transformation of social structure and cultural discourse. Polish society is now enduring a profound alteration in normative order. It is also rocked by the formation of new social relations centered in the recurring practices of production and distribution, power and authority, information and knowledge, religion and the world of meaning.

With all this as a prologue, the work at hand should be read on several levels. At the core, this book will construct a theoretical framework for the post-World War II intersection of systemic contradiction and legitimation crisis in Poland. Through this lens of largely macrostructural and historical forces, we will consider the ensuing mobilization and collective self-creation of the resistance movement known as *Solidarnosc*. This retrospective is not an attempt to uncover new detail, but to synthesize credible knowledge and to highlight forces largely obscured by earlier more dramaturgical and romanticist views. In vital ways, the mass appeal of the Solidarity movement in the 1980s transected occupational and status lines in Poland. However, the very universality of the appeal, while effective at a mobilization level, was doomed to break apart with the fracturing of interests in the institutional phase. For many Poles, especially the industrial workers at the core of the movement, the legitimation of Solidarity was vested in its egalitarian ideals. However, after the seizure of state power, the forces of resistance found themselves on the horns of a dilemma. What can be called the "fast track" to a market system assumed that economic development would follow laissez-faire Polish "marketization." The unstated corollary was that the social price to be paid was greater, not less, inequality. And herein lies the crux of the great and contemporary divide that marks the Polish transformation.

The Polish transformation is not occurring in a vacuum. With historical context in place, we turn in chapter 4 to the positioning of Poland in the new Europe as seen through the prisms of two organizations. OECD (the Organisation for Economic Co-operation and Development) is comprised of the governments of the twenty-four nations that are positioned at the top of the global market system. Its Partners in Transition project offers technical assistance to Poland and other Eastern European states. The project, taken as a whole, offers an instrumentalist view of institution building--with a primary but not exclusive focus on the market economy. For its part, the United Nations Educational Scientific and Cultural Organisation (UNESCO) has sponsored intellectual forums on Eastern Europe for those more interested in the axiological side of change. Taken together, these two visions can be said to represent Western exemplars of the Polish transformation.

These exemplars remain in place, though the hard and difficult years since the Round Table negotiations of 1989 have taught bitter truths to many Poles. But the rise and fall of Solidarity is not simply a Polish or Eastern European lesson. This particular case history is placed in the context of world market forces and the new relations among states and national economies. This wider view remains instructive as the forces at play remain contemporaneous and more powerful than ever. Moreover, the case of Solidarity tells us something about those social movements that are not to be confined to national borders in the coming twenty-first century. Facilitated by a communications revolution that is both unidirectional and interactive and by burgeoning problems and dilemmas that do not recognize lines drawn on maps, what appears to be an internal formation of resistance may easily assume transnational proportions. Whether progressive forces such as today's Greens, who seek sustainable and equitable development, or the repugnant backlash of nativists opposing desperate migrants and immigrants, tomorrow's movements, through ideology or action, will cross borders and shake the world.

Finally, the pages that follow afford the opportunity to ponder the paradox of change. On the one hand, the charismatic leadership, the ideology, and the organizational tactics that serve a movement for change so well may prove detrimental or irrelevant once power is taken. On the other, the course of change may not be a simple movement from domination to freedom or from command stagnation to market prosperity. The latter offers new threats to freedom and dignity. Laissez-faire privatization routinely ignores the central questions of human development, such as sustainability, distribution, and social justice, while relegating the issues of cultural and spiritual richness to a realm outside. The Polish paradox is that these were the very forces that gave birth to Solidarity and sustained the movement in a dark decade of near extinction. It is these forces, in all of their material and moral dimensions, that will have to be recovered and institutionalized in the new Poland.

Acknowledgments

Many have contributed to the work associated with this publication. They include administrators, faculty colleagues and students at both the Uniwersytet Jagiellonski in Krakow and Eastern Washington University. Full cooperation was extended by officials and staff affiliated with UNESCO; the Center for Educational Research, Polish Ministry of Education in Warsaw; the Partners in Transition Program at the Organisation for Co-operation and Development in Paris; and the Parliamentary Assembly and the Division of Pan-European Co-operation Programmes at the Council of Europe in Strasbourg.

At Greenwood Publishing Group, Elizabeth Murphy and James Ice invested both their faith and their editorial expertise. Those invited to review the manuscript included John Foster of the University of Oregon, Louis Gray of Washington State University, Ed Herman of the University of Pennsylvania, Diana Khor of Stanford University, Peter McLaren of UCLA, Raja Tanas of Whitworth College, and Sue Marie Wright of the University of Oregon and Eastern Washington University. Crucial and varied support for the project was extended by Richard Curry, Dean of Letters, Arts and Social Sciences; Neil Zimmerman of the Office of the President; the EWU Foundation; and a faculty grant from Eastern Washington University. Tina Hormel conducted vital library research, and Jane Henson provided invaluable assistance with manuscript preparation. In addition to other formal duties, Dr. Boguslawa Matwijow played a crucial organizational role in Poland and with Dr. Krzysztof Polak proofed the Polish language.

Chapter 1

Systemic Crisis and Social Movements: The Case of Poland

Not Nero, but God, rules the world.

From *Quo Vadis* by Henry Sienkiewicz, who won the Nobel Prize for literature in 1905, at a time when Poland did not exist on the map of Europe.

Through the decade of the 1980s, it is arguable that no movement on the European continent and no struggle for national liberation on a world scale seized the imagination of the West like *Solidarnosc* in Poland. The heretofore unthinkable civil conflict in Eastern Europe offered the highest drama of political theater, ready-made for the Western media's attraction to charismatic leaders with stature and star quality. In the forefront was Lech Walesa, ordinary electrician and son of a peasant, whose leadership defied the power of the Polish party-state. Solidarity's defiance of this surrogate regime was ipso facto a slap in the hidden face of the U.S.S.R.--at that moment still called a superpower, with its institutional fissures yet to crack wide from the stresses of change. On the backstage was Pope John Paul II, a graduate of the *Uniwersytet Jagiellonski* in Krakow, whose election in 1979 was to infuse the Polish secular struggle with sacred symbolism.

The Polish sea change was simplified in much of the Western world as a struggle of good versus evil, democratization versus totalitarianism, sacred values versus empty materialism, self-determination versus external rule. The contradiction was indeed stranger than fiction. In the prime time of Western and media-constructed history, a nationally supported workers' movement, led by a trade union of ever-changing legal status, would defy two self-described workers' states. Correspondingly, the Catholic faith, officially viewed as an agent of mystification, was to be remade in the crucible of nationalism. In the clash between the forces of order and change, the teachings of the faith were redefined by believers as a mandate for temporal justice. Religion was thus transformed from the transcendental to the immanent. The symbols of the faith became those of political resistance, and this process of conversion was to provide *Solidarnosc* with a looming moral authority. However, while there is truth in simplicity, simplification inevitably loses something in translation. As Janine Wedel has eloquently argued:

It is tempting to read this story as a morality play climaxing with the end of Communism, then culminating in a pre-determined, satisfying denouement. It is equally tempting to see Poland's period of "transition" as a messy necessity that inevitably will do away with the evils of the previous system. The tendency of many in the West to assume one particular outcome of the Polish "transition" arises partly from wishful thinking. Before the metamorphoses of 1989 turned Communist steel into scrap, the West cast the drama of Communism's failure into rewardingly "right" and "wrong" sides. Now equally simplifying and ideologizing phrases without adequate referents such as "civil society," "markets," "pluralism," and "transition to democracy" convey an equally reductionist view of the enormously diverse societies of Eastern Europe. (1992:1)

The work before you will no doubt reproduce certain of the errors implied by Wedel. Indeed, it must be noted that among many of Poland's current political leaders and even the intelligentsia, the problematic of ideological absolutism remains, although it assumes a different form. The belief in a bipolar world dominated most of modern social and political thought (East and West) in the postwar era, reflecting the geopolitical formations of superpower rivalry. For those nurtured in bipolarity, the collapse of the U.S.S.R. leaves only one party standing. What Francis Fukuyama (1992) labels the "end of history" assumes that a Western-style system of representative democracy and markets, somehow preordained, is now preeminent. As many Western observers and Poles, at least on the surface, rush to embrace the victor--some ignore what may prove to be a future imperative: a new paradigm for a new order.

The ideological fiction of bipolarity has been real in its consequences. Much of the postwar world--including Eastern Europe--was subject to forms of intervention (military, economic, political, and cultural), in the name of the opposing designs of Moscow or Washington. However, beneath the design of the superpower chessboard were relations that did not and do not correspond well to ideological dichotomies. Ironically, the new states of Eastern Europe will share the frustration of many new states of the southern hemisphere. They must discover their own options in what can only be conceived as a multipolar world.

Simply argued, the danger looms that the fiction of bipolarity will be superseded by arrangements and doctrines founded on the new myth of unipolarity. An alternative view is that the future, as the past, reflects multiple destinations and multiple paths toward them. If there is to be an authentic Polish future, it must by definition be made by the Polish people themselves. Imitated orders, whether imposed from the outside or copied from within, assume the foreclosure of the future. Replications of the past declare that new experiments are not really new at all, that a newly liberated people have little to offer to the mix of human societies. There are still asymmetrical relations here, if not those of physical force and dependency, then those of arrogance and submission. Realizing this, it is the Poles themselves who must decide how and in what ways they shall retain their right to make an authentic future. With this caveat in mind, we now turn to the movement to transform Polish society.

THE DECONSTRUCTION OF SOCIAL MOVEMENTS

Among his nine predictive theses on the future of sociology, Anthony Giddens argues that "social movements will continue to be of prime significance in stimulating the sociological imagination" (cited in Scott, 1990: 1). Such a prediction appears safe enough. However, the rise of Solidarity represents something of an epistemological crisis for the modern sociology of social movements, a crisis that does not spare order, or pluralist or conflict paradigm. Nowhere is this more evident than in the preeminent theory of order: functionalism.

During the 1950s and much of the 1960s, when functionalism dictated not merely the method but also the appropriate subject of sociological research, the reasons for this marginalizing of social movements were clear. To any theory concerned with stability and functionality, social movements were something of a fly in the ointment. They were sources of potential disruption to an entity whose stability, and not instability, was the proper object of analysis. Only by assuming their marginality was the integrity of the theoretical system ensured. (Scott, 1990: 2)

The focus in functionalism on stability has always presented an ideological problem in sociology. Talcott Parsons viewed movements of change as disruptive of grand systems, and conceptually isomorphic with deviance and a breakdown of social control. However, the domain assumptions of Parsonian theory were implicitly grounded in familiar political conceptions of order and change. The ideological nature of this position is clear when Parsons identifies the specific referent of his "civilization" as Western, and specifically in the twentieth century, as the United States (Perdue, 1986: 112-19).

Stated concisely, Parsons and other systemicists/functionalists, such as Neil Smelser, conceive of social movements as a *problem* for social order. However, when the order involved is not Western, something is lost in theoretical translation. Under functionalism, the analysis of movements of social change is bound to evolutionary assumptions. Thus argued, movements for change become problematic when they go beyond the ends of the minimum challenges required to facilitate adaptation, and/or enhance structural complexity and flexibility. Functionalism then, in the context of pre-1989 Poland, could only address by its logic the "problem" of institutional maintenance, in this case the maintenance of the Polish party-state. Conversely, the Solidarity movement would, by the logic of Western functionalism, represent a threat to the party-state and by extension, to the broader sphere of systemic equilibrium. The point is that functionalism assumes that the basis for social order is some sort of consensus and/or cultural integration. Because of such epistemological limitations, this theory is ill equipped to pose the question, Whose order? To the extent that such assumptions of order are compromised, the theoretical utility of functionalism breaks down.

A second paradigmatic crisis in the Western sociology of social movements appears on the pluralist side. By pluralism I mean the view of social order as one of antagonistic cooperation. The image here is one of a heterogeneous society representing perhaps multiple cultures and certainly more than a few interest groups. These groups may be locked in multilayered and asymmetrical relations of power, but larger groups tend over time to introduce a dynamic balance, and the leading interests in one era may be replaced by others who mount successful movements, whether political or cultural.

Viewed through the pluralist prism, movements are often symbolic crusades by which outsiders seek some form of *cultural* affirmation. Political goals, if important at all, are defined in terms of seeking contractual standing in a society seen to consist of reciprocal relationships. Again, what is clearly assumed is a Western model of society rooted in some variety of social contract, in which movements emanate from disaffected interest groups seeking their piece of the pie.

What is usually termed the conflict model in Western sociology at a general philosophical level offers more heuristic assumptions, but when formal varieties of conflict theory are examined, another breakdown is evident. The critical/structural theories founded in the conflict vision assume inequality, coercion, and struggle in the past and present but the coming of a more egalitarian and utopian future through institutional transformation. Given such assumptions, social movements at any moment in time may be committed to progressive emancipation or, under the enabling conditions of archaic ideologies and relations, they may embody the forces of reaction seeking the mythological security of a lost past.

So far, so good. It would appear (at least superficially) that there is some resemblance here to Solidarity as a more progressive emancipatory movement. However, as is usually the case, the devil is in the theoretical details. I will argue that there is a problem of conceptual space separating the realities of the movement from the structure of Western sociological thought. Thus, to comprehend Solidarity is simultaneously a problem in the sociology of social movements and in the sociology of knowledge. As is the case for the order and pluralist paradigms, we shall see that Solidarity as a (former) movement or (present) institutional party also does not "fit" Western assumptions on the conflict side.

Conflict theories in the Western context have routinely focused on the political economy of change, with the structures to be altered once again those familiar to Western order, past or present. Within the context of this paradigm, movements assume one of two forms. The first, and most recognizable, are the class-based movements of the traditional and new varieties of Marxist theory, in which objectively defined economic categories (workers, peasants, the middle classes old and new, a rising commercial elite, etc.) rise in a quest to transform the institutional structure of society. Class movements emerge from a synthesis born of being and consciousness. Thus, objective location or nexus within the relations of class struggle, under propitious historical conditions, coincides with the emergence of a collective and enlightened sense of "we" and "they"- a consciousness that emerges dialectically through struggle. Social movements devoid of class politics, on the other hand,

are a category puzzle, neither fish nor fowl. They have some of the characteristics ascribed to real--that is, class movements (for example, mass mobilization), but they appeal to "illusory" collective identities such as nation, gender, locality, or even, most disturbing of all, to abstractions such as "the public" or "humanity." The temptation to employ the language of "false consciousness" in an attempt to explain, or explain away, non-class-based social movements is one into which much analysis has fallen. (Scott, 1990: 3)

This sort of conceptual reduction of "real" movements to a monistic form (with class relations as the only fulcrum of change) introduces a range of theoretical problems. These include the theoretical negation of such forces as ethnicity/nationality, religious identity, the social psychology of betrayal, and the corresponding conceptual reduction of ideology to consciousness. Outside this domain of the cultural/ideational (politics), the monistic approach to movements (of class) necessarily "demotes" manifestly political struggles that seek the power of the state in other than capitalist-type societies. Or it defines the third world problematic only in terms of external domination by core or lead colonial powers. All of this is not to say that class movements do not or have not existed nor to suggest that internal and external relations of domination implicating market economies have no place in the study of social movements. The point is that other forms and relations of domination, involving the state and civil society, exist and are not reducible to a simple monism of class. This is clear in the case of many national liberation movements in the colonized world, old and new. I will argue that it is also true in the case of Solidarity.

To argue that Solidarity escapes the conceptual boundaries of the critical/conflict and other Western paradigms of sociology is also to challenge the utility of the most recent attempts to develop new thinking on movements. This is because such "new" thinking is also context bound. David Mason (1989), for example, has argued that Solidarity may be considered a "New Social Movement"; however, he does not identify new paradigmatic assumptions or movement criteria that fit the Polish (or other non-Western) situations. The criteria for "new social movements" once again find their origins in social conditions that ring true for wealthier Western nations, but bear only passing resemblance to the institutional and cultural structures of other societies. But, we are getting ahead of our argument. The conception of "new social movements" bears the theoretical imprimatur of Jurgen Habermas and Alain Touraine. We shall begin with the former.

Social movements for Habermas are linked to legitimation crisis in postindustrial societies (1976, 1987). The problematic of legitimation is rooted in the question of authority, and more specifically, the rational political authority of the modern state. On one level, political democracy is legitimate to the extent that the rituals that signify contractual relations and those that symbolize heeding the people's will reproduce mass loyalty. On another level, the expanding and complex role of the modern Western state is to articulate, negotiate, balance, and steer the economy through structurally founded contradictions. Perhaps the most fundamental of these contradictions encompasses the private and egoistic nature of capital accumulation on the one side, and the public and broadly rooted nature of labor--together with the bonding of reciprocity of social relations--on the other.

In more concrete terms, the ongoing struggle for legitimacy marks the quest of the state to maintain the authority of popular consent and to forestall recourse to rule by naked coercion. Yet the popular consent basic to legitimated power (authority in the Weberian sense) cannot be engineered from ideology alone. Whatever one may say about "real democracy," the critical experiment occurs when popular expectations of greater egalitarianism and a societal wide agenda clash with the interests of dominant circles or organizations also funded or subsidized by the state-interests that are seeking to maintain or expand their command and resources. Although there are many roots and nuances, the most profound legitimation crisis is a familiar one. The state

bears the cost of international competition and the cost of the demand for unproductive commodities (armaments and space research); it bears the cost of infra-structural activities directly related to production (transport systems, scientific and technical progress, occupational training); it bears the cost of social consumption which is only indirectly related to production (housing construction, health, leisure, education, social insurance); it bears the cost of social security for the unemployed; and finally it bears the cost of burdens on the environment created by private production. (Habermas,1976: 376)

In his later work, Habermas continues to shift the nexus of conflict away from class relations and the attendant problems of distribution and toward problems of modernity--more generally, the "social malaise which is to be understood in terms of the structural transformation of liberal into late capitalist society" (Scott, 1990:8). Certain of the dimensions of this malaise, though apparently structural in origin, penetrate the cultural and social psychological spheres of shared human existence. Particularly revealing are the dilemmas of "civil privatism." Traditionally, the cultural values and social psychological motivations are manifested in such forms as the stand-alone family, consumption, and the drive for achievement. In the Western context, these conditions contribute to the maintenance of the higher system. However, they are also out of phase with the complexities of modern life and the emergence of a more pervasive and intimate role for the rational state. Correspondingly, the failure of self-reliance, hard work, and personal ambition--to bring rewards and to ensure social mobility--begins to pervade the public consciousness. Promises are broken and aspirations are thwarted. There are chains to be broken here. But for Habermas, they are the chains of modernity.

The new discourse on modernity features the conflicts born of changed social relations in postindustrial society. The problematics now address the problems and perversions of technical rationality that produce an "inner colonization." (Habermas, 1987: 392) Let us take the opportunity to interpret and amplify. In the modern Western order, the new middle classes (often technical/professional workers assumed to be free of the reality or fear of material want) turn their attention toward "noneconomic" intrusions. These include the invasion of authority in the name of efficiency, mindless routine rationalized as productivity, and threats to health and environment in the cause of growth.

Growing disillusionment with such conditions are not expressed in system-specific movements to bring down institutions or to transform the mode of production. Instead, the struggle toward freedom is channeled toward new objectives by means of "new social movements." These new movements are described by Habermas as oriented toward such ends as "quality of life, equal rights, individual self-realization, participation and human rights." The "old politics" in turn galvanizes such groups as "employers, workers and the middle-class tradesman, whereas the new politics finds stronger support in the new middle classes, among the younger generation, and in groups with more formal education (1987: 392).

The conceptual discourse of legitimation crisis has analytic and sensitizing properties that in some ways transcend the limitations imposed by the Western context. Indeed, in due course, we will explore the issue of delegitimation in the Polish situation. But, although there are some grounds for arguing by analogy, the crisis of the former party-state apparatus in Poland is not isomorphic with the crisis of the state under late capitalism. At the risk of introducing a version of historicism, the "old" and "new" politics of movements are based upon a transformation of the labor force that is more true for Germany, the leading national economies of the European Community, and Japan than it is even for the United States. The conceptual gap between the arguments of Habermas and the conditions of the labor force in Poland is even greater. The argument that when basic needs are met, higher ones can be sought is an old one in the social and behavioral sciences. However, despite the interest in axiology among many students of the Polish transformation, it is misleading to ignore real declines in the Polish standard of living and the threat to jobs. Simply put, a conceptual architecture sufficient to explain anti-authority and/or state reformationist movements in the West does not fit the Polish situation.

It is not that nonmaterial ideals were absent in Solidarity. To the contrary, the language of humanistic values, political democracy, and personal growth blossomed in Polish social life. However, the specific conditions that gave rise to Solidarity and the ends it came to embrace can be distinguished from the new movements represented in Europe by such forces as the Greens in Germany (Scott, 1990) or the antinuclear mobilization in France explored by Alain Touraine in 1983. Touraine and his colleagues published their work on the Solidarity movement in the same year, and it is convenient to consider it here.

The work of Alain Touraine is in some respects more pluralist and specifically Weberian due to the theoretical centrality of social action. He and his co-workers make clear their break with the traditional varieties of Marxism and functionalism while embracing the imagery of emancipatory struggle against the forces of domination:

Familiarity with Solidarity should convince us--and one of the aims of this book is to help establish this belief--that men and women are not subject to historical laws and material necessity, that they produce their own history through their cultural creations and social struggles, by fighting for the control of those changes which will affect their collective and in particular their national life. (Touraine et al., 1983: 5)

The imagery employed here is that of participation, choice, ideals, collective will; of the active repudiation of a realm of repression that pervades culture and psyche. The intellectual call, here as with Touraine's work taken as a whole, is to bring human agency back to a position of theoretical centrality; to declare the social authorship of history, and specifically to repudiate the Leninist thesis of a vanguard that "serves to justify the dominance of ideologists and political leaders over the social base" (Touraine, et. al., 1983: 4).

The imagery of conscious, willful, collective action, a minded exercise in the popular construction of reality, pervades Touraine's work and informs the methodology. This book on Solidarity is described as a product of "sociological intervention" intended to reveal the "meaning which the actors themselves attribute to their action" (1983: 7). There are two phases to the intervention--the first being a participatory role wherein researchers actually engaged in dialogue with groups of Solidarity militants in order to introduce hypotheses or interpretations of the movement. Such dialogue was not intended to guide or critique the movement, but to facilitate attempts by members to confront and question interpretations and responses. With the aid of the intervention, members move on to the conversion stage where self-analysis or the search for authentic meaning acquires a life of its own. To amplify, it appears that sociological intervention drives a process whereby the quest for meaning on the part of movement representatives moves from a heteronomous to an autonomous level.

Touraine's is a momentous work fashioned from inside the stream of interpretation and action during Solidarity's fateful years of 1980-1981. In some respects, real actors are seen not as passive readers of a script but as the makers and shapers of history. This said, however, sociological interventionism is subject to the same criticism directed toward other forms of participant observation, perhaps raised to a higher power. The construction of social reality is altered not only by the presence, but in this case by the interlocutory, analytic, and interpretive role of outsiders. This factor alone raises many questions, but two are perhaps most vital, and I will review them now.

As virtually every social movement in history has existed without the presence of sociological interventionists, are there not more naturally occurring accounts, renditions, and interpretations by movement members that may be used to judge consciousness, historical role, and even the conversion to self-analysis? More importantly, why assume a dichotomous social world of subject *or* object, culture *or* structure, consciousness *or* being, interactive social relations *or* systemic forces? Why not place the world of action in the context of institutional contradiction and global crisis?

We speak, of course, with the benefit of hindsight, as more recent events have underscored the need to examine the larger forces of history and structure that were necessary (if not sufficient) conditions for the transformation of Solidarity. Touraine and his colleagues wrote in the pre-glasnost era. In 1983, they followed Jacek Kuron in describing Solidarity as "self-limiting" (1983:64-79). The Touraine team believed that movement aspirations were tempered by the fear of Soviet intervention, as well as by the power of the Polish party-state, the moderating influence of the church and the economic crisis. (Such factors may have contributed to Solidarity's willingness to compromise; a political posture defined as weakness by the regime. This is evidenced in the dissolution of Solidarity by the party-controlled *Sejm*, the lower house of the Polish Parliament, on October 8, 1982.)

However, it is now arguable that the church was not as limiting a factor for change as Touraine believed. Instead, it can be argued that this crucible of Polish culture played a moderate role only on the tactical side (stressing the importance of nonviolence)--and was not a barrier to Solidarity on the strategic (emancipatory) side. Further, the economic crisis, in its turn, increased (rather than limited) disaffection among workers, peasants, and intellectuals. Furthermore, history was to prove that the "international" and domestic forces and conditions were linked--but in ways unforeseen by Touraine or anybody else. It was the decline and fall of the U.S.S.R. in the Gorbachev era that removed the specter of Soviet power from the Polish situation and eliminated this international basis for the self-limiting character of Solidarity.

The crux of this argument is that the isolation of the U.S.S.R. and its satellites in the world market, the failure of COMECON to establish a new and efficient second-world division of labor, the resort to repugnant Darwinian labor policies as the Polish party-state sought to compete--all of these and other forces of higher crisis--must be reviewed. It is certainly arguable that Poles assigned meaning to some of these (or at least their manifestations) in their everyday lives, but those conditions of crisis cannot be reduced to cultural/ideational forms of human negation. It is clear that members of Solidarity acted in a self-conscious fashion to begin to produce the institutions of civil society that would alter the fundamental nature of the archaic Leninist state. However, we must also ask: what were the specific conditions, persons, events, and forces about which meanings were constructed? Solidarity did not arise ex nihilo. And the temptation to see in it a case study designed to resolve the Western academic debate between materialism and idealism may miss the Polish point altogether.

DOMINATION AND ANTI-DOMINATION

The rise of workers in Poland, and the ultimate transformation of a specific struggle to form free trade unions into a general social movement for the wider transformation and emancipation of society, thus requires a distinctive thereotical apparatus. The construction of such an explanatory framework will face more than the usual barriers. First, from the nomothetic side, the general identification of structural and ideological forces must be attempted. The identification of these forces need not assume the form of "laws." What is required instead is a systemic framework that transcends the idiographic isolationism that characterizes many "case study" approaches to the study of social movements. At the same time, it is obvious that the Polish case will present specific challenges to a field enshrouded in a Western weltanschauung.

To begin, Western conceptions of social movements routinely assume the existence of "socially shared activities and beliefs directed toward the demand for change of some aspect of social order" (Gusfield, 1970: 2). While a point of departure, this definition is simplistic and raises more questions than it answers. It also reproduces the Western view of change as more or less compatible with the design of liberal democratic order. To raise the level, let us propose that the explanation and analysis of social movements may begin through the identification of more universal ideal types: those seeking some form of distributive justice within an existing order, whether reactive or progressive; those seeking the revolutionary transformation of institutions; and those seeking separation or independence from an occupying or external power.

In some ways, the Solidarity movement embodied properties consistent with each of these. As implied above (and argued precisely below), the early experiences and demands of the workers were born of a sense of betrayal. Yet, on the social or popular side, the early ideology emerging in the strikes and labor unrest of the pre-Solidarity period expressed grievances firmly rooted in the everyday conditions of toil. The remedies demanded would appear to have posed little initial threat to the continuation of the party-state apparatus. However, the party proved incapable of compromise. This intransigence is not to be explained through typical Western recourse to reified conceptions of totalitarianism. It is true enough that for the regime to have compromised on demands would have been to surrender claims to the moral authority claimed by the party vanguard. But there is more. Despite the power-induced blindness that may lead an elite toward blind self-exoneration, it was clear to all that Poland was in the grip of a profound institutional and legitimation crisis. The fear of concessions was, from the side of the regime, a fear of embarking on the slippery slope of decline. However, in avoiding the slope, the party-state found the precipice.

Summing up, then, the Polish context offers distinctive properties, at both macrosociological and microsociological levels and in the material realm and the world of meaning. These include (1) the relations between Poland and other states of the Soviet orbit and the U.S.S.R. in particular, as well as the broader and often hidden ties between East and West; (2) the unprecedented drive to negate a state command economy connected, in turn, to a powerful center; (3) the formation of a movement agenda equally informed by nationalism and a historical sense of domination; (4) the nature and significance of the Polish brand of civil religion (far more sacred in nature than those of Western nation-states); and (5) the ongoing institutional transformation from command and autocracy--all such social facts and others ensure that Western conceptions of movements and change must be modified, stretched, and often discarded.

With this overview as a base, a theoretical course can now be specified and charted. On one level, it is necessary to identify the higher forces of order and change, domination and resistance--embodied in history, in global and regional alliances, in institutional negation, and in grand systems of legitimation. In this higher framework of structural and ideological crisis, the more intimate dramas of movement mobilization are written and performed. This is the peripheral stage of primary interaction and popular meaning, where broken promises and the shame of betrayal take human form. It is within this sphere that power relations are converted into the discourse of movement life--with altered professions of faith relating to material welfare, new conceptions of social being and reformulations of the meaning of human dignity. No single book, much less a chapter, can give adequate treatment to this range of formations and processes. However, that which follows is neither synopsis or digest. It is rather an attempt to identify forces, to illustrate them through exemplary events, and to render them theoretically concise. This is an exercise in synthesis, not detail.

THE MACROSTRUCTURAL CRISIS

While the past is not necessarily prologue (in the sense of repetition, phases, or stages), it is true that history and consciousness cannot be isolated. The historical complexities of Polish resistance and popular revolt can be said to predate, and in some important ways presage, the rise of *Solidarnosc* by at least two centuries. In 1791, a Polish constitution guaranteed some legal protection and religious freedoms for citizens, while providing for a permanent army and a hereditary throne for the monarchy. This eighteenth-century document has been romanticized somewhat when viewed through the lens of modern nationalism, but it is certainly true that the immediate events of the era conspired against a historical test of Polish constitutionalism. After the war with Russia in 1792-1793, Poland lost territory, setting the stage for General Kosciuszko's ill-fated rebellion. With the defeat of his forces in Krakow in 1794, Russia, Prussia, and Austria divided Poland (1795), signaling the termination of the Polish state. In 1815, the Congress of Vienna created a Kingdom of Poland--but under Russian control. Krakow was made a "free republic" under Austrian "protection."

Poles rose against the Russians in 1830-1831, against Prussia and Austria in 1848, and again against Russia in 1863. Russian domination continued until the Bolshevik Revolution and World War I brought a new opportunity for political independence. In 1919-1920, Polish forces under Marshal Pilsudski opposed the Russian forces culminating in the defeat of the weakened state at Warsaw. The historical space between wars was marred by continuing border clashes with Czechoslovakia, Germany, the Ukraine, Lithuania, and of course, the U.S.S.R. (chronology adapted from Marek Zaleski and Benjamin Fiore, cited in Walesa, 1987: 7-9).

The interregnum in Poland, marked by the real but benign authoritarianism of Pilsudski, ended with the invasion of Poland on September 1, 1939, by the Nazi Wehrmacht. However, the story of wartime Poland cannot be reduced to the simple horror of fascism, exemplified as it was in the extermination of six million Poles, half of them Jewish. Before the month was out, Soviet forces marched into Poland from the East. This military vise, resulting again in the political destruction of Poland, was in keeping with the Nazi-Soviet pact finalized by Ribbentrop and Molotov on August 23, 1939. Such collaboration, intended to alter the map of Europe, was the beginning of a more modern reign of betrayal and terror.

Abraham Brumberg (1983) has argued that postwar Soviet relations with Poland represented to many Poles a new version of the old czarist order. It is not only in the period of Western colonialism that imperialism has worn the disguise of lofty ideals and higher purposes. Between 1939 and 1941, the Soviets occupied eastern Poland and deported a million or more Polish "enemies of the people" to Siberia. When the Nazis turned against the Soviets and invaded the U.S.S.R. in June of 1941, an amnesty was declared. By that point, almost half of the deportees had died. In 1940, over 4,000 Polish army officers were executed in the Katyn forest (Kennedy, 1991: 18-19. It was to be over fifty years later before a new Russian order acknowledged that the massacre had been carried out--not by Nazis but by the Soviets. In 1944, the Soviet army failed to render aid to the Warsaw rising against German occupation forces. It is difficult to erase a history of outrage from the memory of a people. But the domination of Poland was to be given another stinging seal of Great Power approval. At Teheran in 1943, and at Yalta (in February) and Potsdam (in July) of 1945, Poland's place in the postwar order was sealed. The Western powers agreed to recognize the Soviet-aligned Polish Committee of National Liberation (PKNW) as the provisional government of Poland. Thus commenced the Sovietization of Eastern Europe.

This brief chronology is intended less as a primer and more as a basis for understanding the Polish experience with external domination. It should come then, as no surprise to find fertile ground in Poland for the sometimes reified nationalism that rises in the clash between the forces of imposed order and the counterforces of autonomy. The tendency to find and sometimes romanticize heroic figures of resistance is not confined to one nation or one people. (Few Americans, for example, are prone to remember that many framers of the U.S. Constitution were slaveholders.) However, as we shall discover in due course, nationalism, especially when blended with the sacred symbolism of the faith, may introduce its own agenda of problems. Be all this as it may, a long history of rule from the outside is simultaneously a compelling source of social and cultural unification and a means of mystifying a history of resistance and its makers.

To this point, however, we may have done little more than reproduce popular history, whereby the Polish people are somehow ordained to rise against the Soviet Union. Yet the Polish political world was and is not so simple a place. In macrostructural terms, there were precipitating forces at play in the 1960s and 1970s that formed in part the enabling context for the rise of Solidarity. And ironically, certain of those forces reflect the commercial power of the world market more than the political and military power of the old U.S.S.R.

Soviet-style economies were increasingly marginalized in global markets in the postwar half century of their existence. They were crippled by an archaic central bureaucracy staffed by the practice of *nomenklatura* (a sort of nomination of the faithful to positions of authority). And they were committed by default to a heavy-industry model of development--with a correspondingly large and industrialized working class. Hence, it is arguable that Soviet political economy was clearly out of phase with the emergence of a highly technologized world order. It is common in the West today to label the new economic order "postindustrial," but that conception distorts the synthesis of high tech and manufacturing in the world's most powerful national economies.

Since the 1930s, the Soviet bloc had been led by Stalin's conception of industrial modernization, founded on the conviction that resource economies would never rank among the world's Great Powers. However, by the 1960s, global economic history had changed. The new modernity on the material side would now be based more heavily on the power to store, process, analyze, and retrieve knowledge. It was a new world--an information age of computers, satellites, and fiber optics. It was a world from which the Soviet bloc had been excluded by the West, partly for real or invented reasons of national security and partly because of geopolitical rivalry. Some of the exclusion was self-created as the bloc attempted to build an alternative order of collective self-sufficiency. Perhaps no more telling symbol of that vision of modernity exists today in Poland than in the massive steel works at Nowa Huta. Nowa Huta (new foundry, in Polish), a small industrial city built adjacent to Krakow during the Stalinist era, houses the tens of thousands of workers who still toil at the massive iron and steel works nearby. When constructed, the works symbolized the massive industrial grandeur of what Poles derisively came to term "real socialism." The Nowa Huta works today are less a symbol of economic power than a reminder of broken promises. Despite marginal external aid and consultation, Nowa Huta remains as of this writing a source of massive air pollution that attacks health (especially of children and the aging) and eats away at the architectural grandeur of Krakow. Strikes in these works predated, and perhaps presaged, the rise of Solidarity.

Identifying in broad strokes the grand failure of industrial giganticism, however, is not sufficient to set the structural stage for the rise of Solidarity. Other forces were at play. The traditional capitalist, as well as the large landowning class, disappeared under Soviet bloc conditions in postwar Poland. However, Polish peasants resisted the collectivization of farms, insisting after 1945 on a continuation of the land reforms commencing between the world wars under Pilsudski. Their resistance took explicit form in the 1950s, as peasants withheld their produce from markets, creating significant hardships in the cities. The stereotype of Soviet-style collective farming simply did not exist in Poland. A brand of privatization was the rule long before the current movements toward free markets. With the risings of 1956 (which brought the Gomulka "reformist" regime to power), most of the country's farmland was in private hands (Brumberg, 1983). (Over 80 percent of farmland was still privately owned by the time of the momentous events of the 1980s.) However, the transformation of an agricultural society continued at a macrostructural level, with corresponding urbanization in the postwar era. With this transformation of the labor force, former peasants and their progeny thus joined an expanding industrial working class.

At the end of World War II, approximately half the Polish workforce labored in the agricultural sector. By the 1970s, agricultural laborers represented some 30 percent of the total. In the same period, the index of urbanization increased from approximately one-third to over one-half of the population. Also growing were the cadres of scientific, academic, and technical workers deemed essential for a modern economy. It was within this triad of a burgeoning industrial working class, fiercely independent peasants, and the new professionals that the modern formations of Polish resistance were to rise.

The gleaming gigantic factories of the postwar Stalinist era were the engines of Polish economic growth in the 1950s. However, the growth rate dropped from a remarkable level of 18 percent annually between 1950 and 1955 to less than half of that level in 1961-1968 (Laba, 1991: 15). In 1968, party leaders in Poland decided to downshift the model of extensive industrialization, which had continued to absorb massive investment--without corresponding increases in wages, consumption, and improved public benefits. Turning to the CMEA (Council for Mutual Economic Assistance) the Gomulka regime called for a new division of labor among the States of the U.S.S.R. and Eastern Europe to replace the simple cloning of heavy industry in the second world of development. Gomulka warned that Poland was losing ground in the "scientific-technical revolution in which all countries are engaged." (Laba, 1991: 16) His somewhat prescient remarks could well have been generalized to the various states of the East bloc.

But to focus narrowly on the CMEA and the Gomulka regime is to miss the larger sweep of recent history. Michael Kennedy (1991: 11) has referred to the 1970s as an "economic roller coaster," with a boom in the first five years and a bust in the second half of the decade that set the stage for the emergence of Solidarity. However, the higher context for this crisis is to be found in macro level patterns of autarky and dependency. On one horn of this dilemma, one finds the familiar call for collective self-reliance on the part of the old U.S.S.R. and its clients. The dream of autarky proved to be more ideological than material, and to the extent that a socialist division of labor did exist, it bound national economies into a community of dinosaurs. On the other horn, the corresponding attempts to break out of a permanent and growing obsolescence was driven by modernization imperatives--as strong in the ruling circles of the second world as in those of the first. What was to develop in Poland and other states were the conditions of massive debt and uneven exchange in trade so familiar in North-South relations, but ignored in the growing asymmetry of East and West.

The tendency to dichotomize the Polish struggle as one of democracy and markets on the one side and Marxism-Leninism on the other is familiar. However, this encapsulation distorts reality on both horns of the Polish dilemma mentioned above. The ideals and ideology of the Polish party-state offered an interpretation of real socialism that sought to legitimate the ruling party as the embodiment of working class interests and the state as an instrument in the service of global proletarianization (Szkolny, 1981:3). However, it is arguable that whatever the nature of socialist idealism, the function of ideologized Marxism-Leninism in Poland was purely that of legitimation for "real" relations of inherent domination. Even the Polish language revealed the clumsy conceptual reformulation of ideals.

The Polish words for *socialism, socialization and internationalism* (as of 1981) designate respectively the existing social order, state ownership and subordination to the interests of the Soviet Union. The term *anti-socialist* force is used to denote any form of political opposition, while the word *anarchist* is today reserved for those oppositionists who belong to some current of the European socialist tradition. These examples form part of a general phenomenon of *conceptual embezzlement* which reaches deep into the vernacular. This Orwellian process fundamentally limits a people's conceptual framework by rendering inexpressible a whole range of ideas. (Szkolny, 1981: 3)

The criticism (also offered by L. Kolakowski) that socialist ideals simply offered legitimacy to repressive state regimes leads to a more complex conclusion. The state elite and their loyal functionaries would not attempt to develop authentic conceptions, blueprints, and structures for autarky on the foundation of higher ideals. The ideals had themselves been transformed into the means of ideological social control. If we employ the critical semiotics of Roland Barthes, it is arguable that the party-state had sought to establish hegemony in the world of signs--linguistic codes that form the basis for a mediated relationship between the world of matter and the world of meaning. The political mythology of the Polish "vanguard" sought to naturalize hierarchical rule by tying hierarchy to the common good, while the official economic mythology embraced a growth model of modernization. Under the pressure of the ideological apparatus of the state, a socialist division of labor was defined less as a means toward national and (by extension) collective self-reliance and more as a means of facilitating commercial exchange and capital-intensive modernization at both regional and global levels.

As of 1977, researchers at the Institute of Economics of the World Socialist System (USSR Academy of Sciences) made the case for a division of labor among the national economies of the CMEA (formerly COMECON). After extolling the virtues of collaboration as a means toward a higher standard of living for all member countries, the authors argued that the development of an international socialist division of labor was not to be encapsulated within the bloc. The ultimate objectives of the CMEA in a global context were: (1) to stimulate economic and technological development so that member countries would realize enhanced "effectiveness as trading partners", (2) to extend socialist principles to the developing countries, (3) to help stabilize the world economy through planning, and (4) to strengthen the links with capitalist countries "which provide the economic basis for peaceful co-existence" (Shiryaev and Sokolov, 1977: 298-299).

The strength of these links (at a crisis point for Poland's economy) can be quantified. In 1974-1975, the percentage of total foreign trade with market economy countries amounted to 45.4 percent for Romania, 44.4 percent for

Poland, 31.2 percent for the U.S.S.R., 30.9 percent for the then German Democratic Republic, 30.5 percent for Hungary, 26.3 percent for the then Czechoslovakia, and 17.4 percent for Bulgaria (Shiryaev and Sokolov, 1977: 299). A slightly earlier study by Princeton economist Adam Broner (1976) also disputed the widely held view that centrally planned economies were pursuing autarkic trade policies.

During the early 70s, the Polish Ministry of Labor also affirmed its increasing alliances with Western labor ministries. In 1974, W. Kawalec (the Minister of Labor, Wages, and Social Affairs) called for greater cooperation on questions of social policy affecting the rights of workers. It is revealing that in the same document, Kawalec noted that "there has been considerable progress recently in international cooperation in matters of trade, exchanges of know-how, licenses and tourism" (1974: 163). Whatever might be said for international cooperation, it is clear that the ministry (as the regime in general) did not realize that the Polish roller coaster was about to plunge.

It is not the simple myth of autarky that is captivating, however. The commitment to industrial modernization in Poland and throughout the Soviet bloc, together with the drive to participate in capitalist world market trade, had led to a runaway form of technological importation in the form of capital equipment from the West, financed on credit. However, Polish authorities were borrowing heavily, not merely for machinery and equipment, but for raw materials and components necessary for production. Thus the Polish economy was also increasingly dependent on the West for supplies, supplies that were simultaneously digging the trench of international debt.

The rush toward growth in the early seventies also reflected a pattern of trade imbalance. Poland's negative trade gap was only U.S.D. 60 million in 1970, but by 1974, it had grown by some 2,400 percent to a level of 1.5 billion (Kawalec, 1974: 51). In the period 1971-1974, imports from capitalist countries were growing at an average rate of 26.4 percent per annum, while exports to the West grew at only an 8.3 percent rate. Polish goods, at least in the short term, would not compete in the world market. But the overall situation was more complex. From 1973, the world petroleum crisis increased the cost of energy for development. A recession in the West contributed to a restricted market for Polish imports. A gigantic share of national income (perhaps as high as 40 percent) was designated for investment with some three fourths of the total committed to heavy and export industries--a course of action that left Polish domestic demand to be satisfied by expensive imports (Bialer, 1981: 523).

Fearful of the consequences of asymmetrical trade it had presided over, the Gierek regime sought to quell Western imports by command, turning instead toward a policy favoring growth in CMEA trade. The high rates of growth in output during the early 70s (national income rose at over 9 percent per annum from 1971 to 1975) gave way to economic decline, with national income falling by 2.2 percent in 1979 and 4.0 percent in 1980 before plummeting further in 1981 (Blazyca, 1981: 376-77). The handwriting was on the wall. The Polish elite had sought the path of modernization through debt and the acquisition of productive investment and revenues for debt retirement through liberalized trade. They achieved little, but the debt was to remain.

It would be misleading, however, to focus narrowly on the decade leading to the rise of Solidarity. When Gomulka came to power in 1956, the Polish regime had also turned to Western credits to finance a substantial rise in living standards and strong increases in capital investment. When the repayment of those credits came due in the early 1960s, Gomulka introduced austerity measures, with harsh social consequences (see next section), including a range of strikes and revolts that drove him from power in 1970. The Gierek regime was doomed to reproduce the errors of its predecessor.

On the macro level, it can now be seen that the Polish economy was undergoing a relentless process of intermittent absorption into the world market order for a quarter century before the rise of Solidarity. This thesis is so important that we shall explore it from a variety of directions in chapters to come. Despite Gierek's 1976 economic maneuver to end import dependency on the West, the Polish debt to advanced capitalist countries continued to skyrocket. In 1971, it was U.S.D. 1.2 billion, by 1975, it reached 7.6 billion, and by 1980, the debt stood at 23.0 billion (Nuti cited in Kennedy, 1991: 37). As reported by the conservative financial publication *Fortune* magazine (Sept. 9, 1980), the charges and interest associated with the loans to Poland were on a par with those granted to third world debtors also seeking to modernize. By 1979, over 90 percent of Poland's hard currency from exports went toward debt repayment. Price reforms were introduced by the Gierek regime in 1980, at least in part as a precondition for further loans (ibid). The local strikes against these increases were to precipitate one of many legitimation crises for the Polish party-state. But unlike earlier patterns of unrest, this turning point proved to be the beginning of the final stage of party-state control in Poland.

BROKEN PROMISES: THE DELEGITIMATION OF STATE AUTHORITY

Everyone sent here from Moscow is either a jackass, a fool or a spy.
Adam Mickiewicz, *Dziady*

The history of institutional order, popular resistance, and social change does not correspond to a linear model. However, to provide some sense of theoretical orientation, a distinction must be drawn between a Habermas-style legitimation crisis and a broader pattern of systemic collapse--often hidden behind the facade of narrowly conceived struggles for political authority. In the previous section, an effort was made to introduce a historical view of the Polish situation at a regional and global level and to raise the issue of second-world dependency. This review provides some sense of systemic crisis that goes beyond the convenient demonization of the Soviet Union on ideological and/or nationalistic grounds. This is not intended to deny or minimize the Soviet factor. It is to argue that a reductionist view of external influence, which ignores the problems of modernization related to ties with Western institutions, is an ideological choice, not an intellectual one. If the analysis here is accurate the problems of debt, dependency, trade imbalance, and uneven exchange, along with new patterns of foreign ownership and control, may not vanish with the old U.S.S.R. The clear and present danger is that misdevelopment, with a broad range of related social problems, will continue to march under the banner of "productive investment" in Poland.

It can now be argued that Poland between 1945 and 1989 faced two varieties of systemic crisis in international relations: one well recognized (that of the Soviet-led CMEA with its dinosaur model of industrial development), and the other camouflaged (the ties between command and demand economies at both national and multilateral levels). However, as already hinted, both the apparent crisis and the hidden crisis were evidenced in regime behavior, ultimately leading to a legitimation crisis. The apparent (and popularly conceived) crisis at the regime level was one of party-state totalitarianism with an incompetent face. The hidden crisis was one of external dependency and the internal degradation of labor, but with a socialist face.

It can be said that the legitimation crisis of the Polish state was in fact a series of crises in which the normative legitimacy of the regime was called into question - more or less commencing with the rise of Gomulka to power in 1956. However, the outcome of a legitimation crisis may follow one of two roads: that of relegitimation or that of delegitimation. The road of relegitimation is typically associated with widely promised reforms, perhaps including an actual change in regime command. Delegitimation implies a repudiation of state authority, and thus it is that a changing of the guard is insufficient grounds for resolution of the crisis. Conversely, systemic crisis implies that a higher constellation of forces are at play that are anterior to political solutions alone.

The crisis in legitimacy for the Polish state can be termed cumulative, both in terms of its intensification over time and because of the building of a collective memory among those whose hopes for justice through reform were dashed time and again. Michael Kennedy (1991: 25-32) offers a chronology of events beginning early in the postwar period. W. Gomulka, who had been imprisoned in 1950 for nationalist positions, was released from prison in 1954, one year after the death of Stalin. The tide of relative reform under Nikita Khrushchev had set the regional stage for the deconstruction of Stalinism. The implications for Poland were dramatic. In April of 1956, 28,000 people were granted amnesty and political prisoners by the hundreds were freed. Intellectuals began an attack on the repression of thought and discussion, and the universities joined the battle for academic freedom. Workers insisted on electing trade unions by ballot. Poland lingered under a disastrous plan that had subordinated consumer products to capital goods and now created broad resentment. Attempts at collectivization now produced peasant revolts. And in June, tens of thousands of demonstrators hit the streets in Poznan. They were met with tanks, planes, and military steel. Seventy-four people died, and four hundred were hospitalized. A wave of strikes swept the land.

Gomulka emerged from the Seventh Plenum of the Polish United Workers' Party (PZPR) Central Committee, convened shortly after the debacle, as the leader of a reform faction. Consolidating his power as first party secretary, he presided over a purge of hard-liners, including the Soviet-sponsored minister of national defense, Konstantin Rokossowski, who returned to Moscow, taking perhaps thirty generals and thousands of other officers with him. Whether Gomulka was courageous in opposition to Soviet might or the beneficiary of the softer Khruschev era is beside the point. A victim of Stalinism, he appeared to defend Poland and offer a new era of independence.

Early on, the regime offered what appeared to be widespread political and cultural liberalization. Under the "revisionist" climate, the various movements that had spontaneously taken initiative continued to drive the transformation of 1956. Peasants were the beneficiaries of privatized agriculture, workers' councils flourished, and intellectual criticism took off. Gomulka had little to do directly with these movements, but with his regime came the abolition of the security police, the establishment of a church-state commission, and a change in the new five year plan to emphasize consumer goods and services. After a short period of reformist seduction, however, the formal engagement was terminated well in advance of a marriage between state authority and wider institutional liberty.

The higher systemic context in which the regime operated has been reviewed above. However, the rescinding of the Polish variety of glasnost was to leave a bitter taste. Within a few months to years, liberals (such as W. Bienkowski) within the leadership ranks of the party were forced from influence. Travel was restricted, and the progressive Workers' Council Law of 1956 (which mandated autonomy for councils) was negated by a 1958 law bringing into existence a party-controlled Conference on Workers Self-Management. Independent expression was repressed again, and the promise of economic decentralization emerging from the Seventh Central Committee Plenum of 1956 strangely dematerialized in its implementation. Gomulka, who had used the legitimation crisis of 1956 to gain power, had broken with Stalinism and distanced Poland from Moscow. He had not broken from the hegemony of the party-state. And Moscow, though from a distance, continued to cast a long shadow.

In symbolic terms, Gomulka's rise must be understood in terms of its self-limiting factors. At this first crucial stage, the legitimation crisis was defined in terms of a revolt against the most objectionable features of the old Stalinist order and the continuing legacy of the Russian threat to Polish nationalism. It was not that the new regime offered institutional transformation - no one was calling for some new synthesis, much less Western-style democracy or capitalism (though Gomulka would soon take the road of international market trade.) It was instead believed that this new regime would allow the assertion of the forces of nationalism and religion; the movements of workers, peasants and intellectuals for greater autonomy; and a new allocation of resources to raise the standard of living. Historically, the Gomulka era stands as a test of party-state revisionism. Its failure would remain a part of the collective memory of the Polish people.

The 1960s were years of turmoil, as party reforms promising freedom of expression lost all legitimacy with Polish intellectuals. In 1964, two future advisors of Solidarity (Jacek Kuron and Karol Modzelewski) published a critique of the central bureaucracy that foretold the inevitability of a revolution of workers directed toward the ruling elite. Both men served prison terms. Also in 1964, a group of Polish intellectuals signed a letter of protest complaining to the prime minister of the continued reign of censorship. Over a dozen signatories found later that official avenues of publication were closed for their work. The party responded to the criticism of philosophers Leszek Kolakowski and Krzysztof Pomian by their expulsion. In the spring of 1968, a wave of university demonstrations was directed toward various manifestations of censorship (including the closing in Warsaw of the 1831 play by Adam Mickiewicz, *Dziady*). Student and faculty demonstrations swept Krakow, Wroclaw, Poznan, Lublin, and, quite prophetically, Gdansk. The Gomulka regime responded with a diversionary anti-Semetic campaign. When students occupied a building at Warsaw University in March of 1968, the party-state reacted by imprisoning student leaders, expelling 1,600 students, eliminating academic departments, and dismissing faculty, administrators, and revisionist party officials (Kennedy, 1991: 33). The Warsaw Spring ended much as did the Prague Spring of the same year, with Soviet tanks in Czechoslovakia firing shots heard in Poland and around the world. For its part, the Gomulka regime had sent in Polish troops as part of the Warsaw Pact forces. In Prague, it became apparent that totalitarianism was not to have a human face. However, looming above the cultural and political crisis was the omnipresent economic crisis.

As intimated above, the end of the decade found the Gomulka regime skeptical of the East bloc call for a more rational division of socialist international labor. Accordingly, the Polish state in 1969 adopted certain domestic policies in an attempt to resolve the economic crisis and free capital for new investment (Laba, 1991: 16-18). On the entitlements side, the regime embarked upon a course of sharply reduced spending on housing, health care, and other services and (in late 1970) introduced drastic price increases in basic food staples. Coupled with the ongoing inflation in the costs of consumer goods (often in short supply), this move raised the specter of deprivation for even the most basic of necessities. However, it was another strategy that proved more specifically fateful for the channeling of the mass energy of discontent.

The Gomulka regime also undertook a painful program of targeting certain industries for development and others for shrinking or closure. *Among the latter was the shipbuilding industry.* More generally, the regime introduced its own Darwinian conceptions of labor, which blamed workers for what it crudely defined as a crisis in productivity. The regime and aligned *nomenklatura* made the claim that some 80 percent of the workday was not rationally utilized, while preparing to accept a 5 percent level of unemployment to put unproductive workers "under the gun." In May of 1970, the Central Committee offered a new five-year plan in which overtime was limited and wages and other compensation were set at existing levels for at least two years. Correspondingly, party unions and managers took up the campaign of blaming the victims. Workers, who had borne the brunt of the crisis, were now labeled as officially responsible for their own increasing misery.

In effect, the state-party apparatus had attempted to absolve those in power from responsibility for the rupturing structural contradictions. This was transparent to those on the downside of asymmetrical power relations who were actually doing the work. However, it is somewhat striking to note that a very similar ideology of worker-blaming permeates the view of certain Western development organizations, as well as some Polish economic, political, and academic circles in the New Poland. This historical replay will be explored at a more appropriate juncture. For now, suffice it to say that the ideological portrayal of slothful workers, and the accompanying draconian plans for the elimination of inefficient industries were important preconditions for the labor strikes and revolts that were ultimately transformed into a resistance movement.

Among the industrial sites *not* chosen for modernization in 1969 was the Lenin Shipyard in Gdansk, already weakened by the general malaise and the decline in capital investment. In global terms, the Gomulka regime saw itself to be prescribing the bitter medicine leading to profitability and, at some future point, a competitive niche in the world market. The official Polish economic solution was to jettison deadweight, with the Lenin Shipyard both an inviting and a symbolic target. It was here that state/party planners foresaw a sea change in Polish economic history. They were right about change but wrong about its sociohistorical direction. The forces unleashed by these decisions were not those anticipated. The yard's workers defined the situation as one of human exploitation. To them, the ideological side of the legitimation crisis was clear. The workers in a workers' state were to be expendable. For their part, the party "unions" were defined not as the defenders of workers' rights but as the executioner's sword.

The Gomulka regime had survived the intellectuals' revolts of the 1960s, but it was not to survive a workers' revolt. Precipitating events included the price rises of December 12, 1970, as well as a change in the scale of industrial wages. In Gdansk on December 14, a strong demonstration occurred near the shipyards. On December 15, ten thousand people protested, and the main railway station and regional party headquarters went up in flames. On December 16, workers marched from the shipyards. They faced armored tanks with flesh and blood. After a surge of strikes that paralyzed much of the Baltic coast and Warsaw, a general strike was called on Monday, December 21. Gomulka's call for Soviet support was ignored by Brezhnev (Kennedy, 1991: 35).

One might speculate that two factors were involved in Brezhnev's decision. On the one hand, the Gomulka regime began with a repudiation of Soviet intervention in Polish affairs. Now the Soviets repudiated Gomulka. On the other, the wave of unrest in peasant, intellectual, and now workers' circles demonstrated no evidence of a renunciation of Soviet-style political economy. The target was a specific regime. It proved once again to be an easy matter to change the guard. On December 20, 1970, Edward Gierek assumed the position of first secretary of the party.

The Gierek regime's macroeconomic strategy of modernization through debt was analyzed earlier. However, the more immediate and transparent legitimation crisis was political and requires some understanding of regime tactics and betrayal. On the tactical side, Gierek pursued an early policy of negotiation and consultation with the workers who had brought down Gomulka--by demonstrating their strength through continuing strikes and threats of strikes. The "wage reforms" of Gomulka fell first, victims of a January occupation strike by the Warski shipyard workers in Szczecin. In the following month, a strike by ten thousand women textile workers in Lodz brought about other consultations with Gierek. With this and other strikes in progress, Gierek rescinded the price increases of December that helped spark the rising against Gomulka. In cumulative retrospect, it is clear that these events had proven that workers had the power to force concessions, a lesson that was not lost on either side. However, it is also true that worker mobilization and a broader social movement against party-state authority had yet to form. In this sense, the Gierek regime had dodged the bullet. For the moment, the legitimation crisis had been resolved by relegitimation.

Gierek quickly demonstrated that concessions on prices and wages did not mean concessions on structural change along democratic and participatory lines. The regime reneged on its promise of an independent workers' commission at the Szczecin shipyards, and the promised consultation took the form of lectures by party officials. However, the debt-financed boom of the early 70s perhaps did more to quiet the resistance than regime force and intimidation. When trade earnings proved illusory by mid-decade, the regime took two drastic steps to attempt to satisfy its creditors: it exported food needed by the Polish people and then (in June of 1976) raised prices on consumer goods. The latter decision was rescinded in response to outbreaks of strikes, demonstrations, and riots (Szkolny, 1981: 12-13).

Undoubtedly inspired by the example of workers' resistance and their power to wring concessions, some Polish intellectuals opened a second front. A small group of ten or so formed the Committee for the Defense of the Workers (KOR) in September of 1976. The official program of the committee was to support the families of imprisoned workers. The covert purpose was the formation of an alliance of resistance. Many intellectuals and students, though never formally among the thirty or so members who comprised KOR by 1980, rallied to develop the weapon of ideas. Underground newspapers and pamphlets began to proliferate, including the famous *Robotnik* (The Worker). This was not merely an intellectual organ. Workers were heavily involved in its production.

Out of the hundreds of worker militants who were drawn into the web of activity around *Robotnik* there coalesced several independent foci. One such was formed by a group in Gdansk in April 1978, who designated themselves as "The Founding Committee of the Baltic Free Trade Union." The historic importance of this group may be judged from the fact that it included at least five of the nineteen members of the presidium of the inter-enterprise strike committee in August 1980, one of whom was Lech Walesa. (Kennedy, 1991:14)

A final dimension of the recurring cycle of legitimation crises faced by the Polish party-state extends beyond political repression. It can be labeled a "crisis of competence" and is of crucial importance in the contemporary sense. While not as dramatic as the brutality of tactics used to silence and break workers, the portrayal of state managers as a class of incompetent technocrats came to constitute a powerful imagery of delegitimation throughout Poland. As long as questions of competence are based on particular personalities and specific regimes, legitimation crisis can always pass by replacing the leadership. However, when the critique of command generalizes to the level of structural roles, then personalities and tactical issues are irrelevant to more substantive solutions. There is nothing mystical about the process. When legitimation crisis becomes more or less permanent, as revealed in the futile changing of regimes whose tactical responses inevitably fail, legitimation crisis then stands to be redefined as only symptomatic of a deeper structural malaise.

In summation then, over the decades, the tactics of relegitimation were implemented and exhausted. At a macro level, Gomulka had sought to distance Poland somewhat from the military industrial policies and archaic Stalinist conceptions of modernization. This had led only to attempts to curtail shipbuilding, aviation, and steel and to remodernize on the backs of workers. On another front, Gomulka had relied on Polish nationalism (expressed in standing up to heavy-handed Soviet intervention) while unleashing, and then smashing, expectations of cultural and political diversity. Among the ironic lessons learned from these early debacles was that there were limits to Soviet intervention; thus revolt within such limits was not suicidal. Successive revolts were to redefine these limits.

The Gierek regime introduced different schemes and tactics which demonstrated that despite the ready availability of force, the party-state danced to both internal and external forces.

After Gomulka, economic policy was hostage to particular industrial and party lobbies, to peripheral and self-interested advice and direction from Western banks and corporations, to the veto of Polish workers, and finally, to the investment priorities established by the Soviet Union. The party's administrative performance --erratic, incompetent, and corrupt--exacerbated these maladies. (Laba, 1991:93)

In a structural sense, the Gierek regime was only playing for time even during the boom years. Aviation, shipbuilding, and Soviet-inspired steelworks (including Katowice) became once again, favored industries. However, growth was fueled not by exports but by credits and imports. There were no structural changes in planning and management, investment projects were left unfinished, there was little improvement in productivity, and one of the most important Polish products became waste (Bialer, 1981: 525-26). Despite a regime drumbeat of industrial power and modern success, the truth was that Poland could sell only primary products and agricultural goods under the conditions of the competitive world market. During the 1970s, with a quarter of the workforce engaged in agricultural production, Poland used six billion U.S.D.

in credits to import food (Laba, 1991: 93).

Jean Woodall identified a series of regime tactics in 1981. Although she presents these simply as antecedents for the "unrest" in Poland at the time, the failures demonstrate preconditions that were to raise the issue of crisis from a particularistic conception of regime incompetence to a more generalized conception of institutional contradictions.

    1. Party-state managers remained committed to a "big is beautiful" model of industrial development, with 75 percent of industrial output in large-scale production units by 1977. The rationale was that such enterprises would make possible "economies of scale in production, research and development, marketing and supplies" (1981:42). The reality of big state corporations also meant big managements unable to respond to demand, and cumbersome organizations that proved inefficient and monopolistic.

    2. Contrary to the official ideology of equality and moral incentives, central planners after 1950 had relied heavily on material incentives in the form of performance bonuses for workers and managers. Furthermore, larger and/or more profitable enterprises could afford to invest more in social facilities for the workforce and their dependents (medical services, nurseries, sports and recreation, etc.). Such a system was to breed inequality and resentment. Incentives were designed to stimulate productivity in the capitalist sense of scientific management. Workers in less successful enterprises believed they were penalized through no fault of their own - leading to a growing sense of betrayal. When the higher productivity of some enterprises resulted in some subsidization of the less productive, more productive workers also lost faith.

    3. Woodall notes that the key to managerial power in Polish industry was a degree in engineering, not business training-although new management training centers were established to develop Western techniques of business administration (1981: 43). (Certainly in the West, and today in Poland, the absence of such training is seen to be a fundamental and historical reason for the incompetence of Polish managers, and thus the premium on business education. We shall assess the limitations of this view at a later point). There is a structural point to be drawn from her description of this situation, however. With the Directors Charter of 1972, more and varied Western-style layers of management were created at the senior, middle, and clerical level - to work at levels below the chief directors of large enterprises. As bonuses were much more generous for management, lower posts were actively sought out by white collar workers whose numbers were increasing in a manner in keeping with the new model. Hence, a growing cadre of more privileged workers coexisted with calls for enhanced productivity (speed-ups) and wage controls for those doing the work.

Stated simply, the Polish party-state in the 1970s was busy producing a bizarre synthesis of Leninist one-man management to ensure party rule with a Western-style managerial model promoting the hyperdevelopment of a privileged white collar surplus class. It was this new class that received a larger share of enterprise earnings than did the increasingly degraded Polish working class. This structure represents more than a mechanism for inefficiency and incompetence. It is yet another dimension of a breach of faith. Frank Parkin, in his seminal work on inequality in command and market systems, made the point over twenty years ago.

It is not too fanciful to assume that continuous and systematic exposure to the tenets of Marxism-Leninism has encouraged a more widespread commitment to egalitarian values than is the case in capitalist society. However, by this same token, if the "official" values of socialist society lay heavy emphasis on equality and classlessness, then any drive towards large-scale inequality is liable to produce serious tensions. At least the working class in capitalist society is not tantalized by formal claims concerning its historical destiny, innate dignity and the like. (1972: 163-64)

As early as 1981, the Polish conflict was being revealed as something beyond a simple polarization of an industrial working class on the one side-and an increasingly delegitimized party apparatus on the other (Woodall, 1981: 46). The Polish imitation of capitalist management structure and rewards was mixed with party hegemony, thus compounding the contradictions of stratification. The situation was made more complex by the simultaneous occurrence of patterns of manual labor degradation, coupled with the rapid expansion of educational opportunities. Stated simply, education was increasingly defined in Poland as a means of workplace advancement. In particular, the expansion of higher education, intensified since the late 1960s with the Polish postwar baby boom, produced more highly trained people who were trapped in lower management positions.

This chapter of party-state delegitimation reflected the double contradiction in the Polish stratification system. First of all, education for advancement redefined learning as instrumental and careerist. This has the usual degrading implications for the philosophy of education, but also creates expectations that encounter structural barriers. The familiar labor market dilemma of overqualification may be redefined as a form of underemployment, wherein the production of managerial personnel exceeded the production of managerial positions. At the same time, the linking of higher education to advancement could only increase the resentment of the younger cadres toward older, politically connected managers with better jobs and less formal training.

One final example will demonstrate the overall complexity of party-state delegitimation. Poland as of 1975 was marked by regional inequalities. However, regional equity goals were not important in the postwar drive toward reconstruction. Efficiency was instead emphasized, with growth presented as the key to the lifting of backward regions (Zimon, 1979). It is clear that the ideology of growth was as fundamental a force in command-style modernization as in the market-driven West. In neither system could it be demonstrated that the benefits trickled down. However, in Leninist states, the triumph of national growth objectives over the official ideology of a more equitable distribution was another episode in betrayal. Thus it can be argued that uneven development was an element of the Polish party-state legitimation crisis. In official ideology, uneven development was the plague only of a dependent and neocolonized third world. Its manifestations in Polish regional inequalities were now to mock the masters of the state.

To this point we have attempted to grasp the higher forces of political economy reflected on the side of Polish institutional power--before the birth of Solidarity. However, the preconditions for the transformation of consciousness are necessary but insufficient to explain the rise of the resistance forces. In the chapter to come, we turn to the forces of change that emerged to challenge the party-state and the broader constellations of regional power, with the U.S.S.R. at the center.

THE DISCOURSE OF BETRAYAL

In the development of a consciousness of resistance, it is essential to realize that a ready-made and full-blown trade union ideology did not simply emerge as some positivist effect of natural causes. Through grappling with specific conditions of struggle embodied in recruiting and organizing; through torturous negotiation; through coming to terms with the history of a nation; through the hard taskmaster of realpolitik, Polish workers and their allies were to come of age. But be this as it may, the pre-Solidarity social and political consciousness of the Polish workers and the Polish people were shaped in a crucible of betrayal. A pervading sense of betrayal did not rely on the formal study of trends in past events, but was rooted in real life experience. This consciousness of betrayal can best be understood as cumulative, historical, and often first person. While we have traced the material events behind this breach of faith, its permeation into a new language of resistance is revealed in a strike bulletin issued by *Solidarnosc* on August 27, 1980:

> *Gentlemen! You are talking to different people.*
>
> *You are not addressing those who in December 1970 replied to the question "Will you help us?"with the answer "We will!"*
>
> *We are different above all because we are united and no longer powerless.*
>
> *We are different because thirty years have taught us that your promises are not kept!*
> (cited in Szkolny, 1981: 19)

The Polish response to the legacy of internal and external betrayal was to shake the states within the Soviet orbit - and ultimately the world. We turn to the politics of betrayal in the chapter to come.

Chapter 2

Solidarity: From Resistance to Transformation

There is a tendency in some quarters to describe Poland under the old Soviet hegemony as one-sided tyranny; as a communist revolution imposed from above. Given this dichotomous thesis of tyranny and freedom, resistance would become little more than a natural response, mounted simply by those yearning for autonomy. As explored in chapter 1, this romanticized view represents an evasion of complexities. A twisted model of debt and dependency, unequal trade relations, and archaic Soviet-style industrial development constituted the higher forces of systemic crisis. Such macrolevel dynamics were the context for a legitimation crisis at the political level, manifested in more clearly recognized and resented contradictions--of privilege and superfluous management, of vacuous secularism backed by the threat of force and by a range of other party-state behaviors revealing both incompetence and a breach of faith.

However, in the pages to come, it will be revealed that there is more to the Polish story than a bumbling and brutal party-state acting to provoke long-standing animosities among Polish sacred nationalists. Here, the story of the opposition, occupying the subordinate side of asymmetrical relations of power, will be told. The story will take the form of the emergence, maturation, and transformation of a movement revealed in deed and word, in ideology and action. Stated clearly, the Polish workers' movement became a national movement, and the quest for trade unionism became a struggle for new institutions waged by an expanding alliance of Poles.

Shaped internally by the dynamics of movement building and externally through conflict and negotiation, Solidarity advanced and stalled and advanced again. Touraine has advanced the thesis that those most committed to the movement were ever mindful of Soviet intervention, ever wary of party-state power, ever suspicious of the dedication of new converts. Indeed, it appears that the movement was to be self-constrained at critical moments by the fear of going one demand too far. But through it all, the movement survived the early success and the crushing martial law of the 1980s. In the final analysis--it endured. However, it also changed internally, and this crucial development will be given attention in due course.

The presentation of Solidarity as a social movement will be informed by a series of principles designed to raise the account that follows - from the level of narrative to one of analysis and explanation. To begin, Max Weber (cited in Parkin, 1972: 161) argued the necessity of assessing the "degree of transparency"; that is, the extent to which structures of domination are easily identifiable to those below. In the Western world, the origins of inequality and betrayal may be well hidden. Thus, some can be expected to define the problem to be changed as coming from one or more of a variety of organizational sources, which in the real world act on a variety of levels. Thus, movement-based politics of protest may be directed toward economic targets (such as specific corporations or employers), governments (at the national, state, or local levels), or even the educational order.

Overwhelmingly, Western movements are directed toward ends that are particularistic and reformist, not holistic and transformational. On this point, the history of U.S. labor reveals the complexity of the transparency issue. In the United States, a clear distinction can be drawn between the pure and simple unionism advocated by the old American Federation of Labor under the leadership of Samuel Gompers, and with the more radical vision of the Industrial Workers of the World. What was to emerge as the AFL began in Philadelphia in 1881 when delegates to the Federation of Organized Trades and Labor Unions of the United States and Canada convened. At this point in North American labor history, the organizational predecessor of the American Federation of Labor (AFL) was distinctive by virtue of its advocacy of a fair share for labor to be achieved within the framework of the existing economic order. Accordingly, its declaration of principles called for

1) Legal incorporation of trade and labor unions; 2) compulsory school attendance; 3) the banning of child labor for those under fourteen; 4) apprenticeship laws; 5) the national eight-hour legislation; 6) against the competition of prison labor; 7) against the truck system; 8) the legal right of the workers to the fruit of their labor through wage demands; 9) repeal of the conspiracy laws; 10) creation of a national labor bureau; 11) a protective tariff for American industry; 12) a ban on importation of contract labor; and 13) the use of the right to vote to send representatives from the trade associations to legislative bodies. (Foner and Chamberlain, 1977: 263-264)

The AFL was to be distinctive in its aversion to strikes, an adherence to elitist (craft versus unskilled) conceptions of workers as opposed to a unitary class, and its "nonpolitical" stance which focused on the threats of immigrant (especially Chinese) and contract labor. There were contemporaries of the AFL who entertained a wider view, however. When the AFL refused to support a strike by the Leadville miners in 1896, the Western Federation of Miners withdrew to organize the Western Labor Union. From this beginning emerged the Industrial Workers of the World in 1905. Certain of the specific demands of the IWW were identical with those of the AFL. However, taken as a whole, IWW demands were seen as means to structural ends. In contrast to the conservatism of pure and simple unionism, the Wobblies called for the emancipation of labor and an ultimate socialist transformation. While the AFL ultimately won the support of those in high places, the "Wobblies" were brutally repressed in one of the more tragic episodes in U.S. history. Leaders were deported or tried and jailed on the basis of political views. In Chicago during the first World War, 100 Wobbly defendants were convicted of conspiracy against the draft and against industrial production (Wolfe, 1978: 22-25). The IWW was essentially broken after less than two decades of existence; however, its radicalism can be viewed as essential in forcing the acceptance of a more conservative unionism on U.S. industrialists and leaders of state.

Viewed through a Weberian prism, the Wobblies can be said to have acted against "the given distribution of property or the structure of the concrete economic order" (Parkin, 1972: 161), because these conditions were deemed responsible for unbearable consequences in their own lives. However, what was transparent for the IWW was opaque for the AFL, because of the apparent fragmentation and multiplicity of the institutional world. For the AFL, it was not a ruling class but specific employers and sometimes industrywide targets that were specifically responsible for unfair labor practices. Correspondingly, the state was defined as a potential ally, not as an organized political instrument of concentrated wealth.

While this historical juxtaposition drawn from U.S. labor history continues to inform theoretically, it also suggests a polarization that denies the complexities of the role of workers in market economies. The active participation of workers in decisions that affect the workplace is generally known as industrial democracy. In tactical terms, the means of industrial democracy form an ideological and political continuum, specifying degree of participation and the security thereof under the authority of the state. The more conservative forms of trade unionism ensure narrowly defined issues of wages, hours, and working conditions founded in legal rights to organize and bargain collectively. This ideal type of pure and simple unionism continues to typify the U.S. model today, although an occasional union leader may occupy a minority seat on a board of directors. The weakness of U.S. unions can be simply demonstrated historically and comparatively. Around 1970, some 30 percent of private sector workers belonged to unions. In 1990, the figure was 12.1 percent. In Sweden the figure is 96 percent, in the U.K., 50 percent, in Germany, 43 percent, in Canada, 36 percent, and in Japan, 28 percent (Hoerr, cited in Perdue, 1993b: 553).

In national economies where union power is stronger, the mechanisms of industrial democracy are more commonly found. The legally insured right to participate in more broadly defined workplace decisions may extend to work councils, existing in much of continental Europe. In a number of European countries (notably Germany and Austria), codetermination law provides for employees' representation on company boards of directors and an actual share in decision making. German "codetermination law requires that half of the board of directors of each large corporation be elected by labor, with the stockholders represented by the other half" (Leontief, cited in Skolnick and Currie, 1991: 368).

The final form of industrial democracy would be workers' control, which in a market economy must be first translated into actual forms of worker ownership. In the United States, capital-starved corporations are often subject to an infusion of pension funds, but such investments are far from representing a controlling interest. Corporations do seek to direct workers' retirement payments from both employers and workers into company stock, make profit-sharing payments in the form of stock, offer inducements for participation in stock purchase plans, offer stock to ease the pain of wage and benefit cuts, and offer stock option programs. Blasi and Kruse have argued that (as of the late 1980s) some 10.8 million U.S. workers owned a bit more than 12 percent of the stock of some 1,000 public companies (Hoerr cited in Perdue, 1993:561).

Ironically, it is the specter of economic crisis in the United States that has driven a more authentic form of worker's ownership. Employee Stock Ownership Plans (ESOPs) are more frequently introduced to save the jobs of workers through some form of employee buyout of existing operations. These plans have increased from 1,601 in 1975, involving only 248,000 workers, to 9,870 plans involving 11.2 million workers in 1990 (United States Bureau of Census, 1992: 534). U.S. unions are skeptical if not opposed to ESOPs, whose existence and proliferation during the deindustrialization of the seventies and the harsh years of Reaganomics confirmed the weakness of unions in U.S. industrial relations. It is also true that ESOPs routinely substitute stock ownership in the enterprise for other retirement investments and subject the "employee-owners" to greater risk.

However, one example of an atypical alliance between unions and the ESOP strategy can be cited. Throughout the 1980s, severe recessions brought scores of metallurgical businesses to the point of bankruptcy. The United Steelworkers, in something of a desperation move, used ESOPs to allow workers to--in effect--buy a chance to remain employed. The union also arranged for ESOP partnerships with management in companies that were still viable. "As of early 1991, the union was involved in ESOPs at 25 companies, many of which are majority worker-owned. The companies range in size from fewer than 50 to 4,000 workers (Hoerr, cited in Perdue, 1993: 561). Whatever the future of ESOPs and other forms of employee ownership in the United States, it is clear that workers and their unions are a long way from authentic industrial power.

The complexities of Western-style industrial democracy do not end with this typology. The Weberian question of transparency is refracted through the myriad of philosophies and ideologies, movements and organizations, core values and categorical interests that make up civil society. It is not enough for workers in Western society to develop a consciousness of betrayal. The mobilization of those with deep and abiding grievances into some form of rational association for action introduces intricate questions of responsibility, short-term tactics, long-term goals, and a myriad of related concerns. All of these in turn are disguised by layers of mystification and force--and driven by the prospect or reality of negotiated rewards for those who persevere, or who are perhaps simply fortunate. The hard-fought winning of rewards thus represents the success of particular movements and often their institutionalized representation in state and economy. The price of the success is often, then, the splitting off of the fortunate from those left behind, a modern form of divide and conquer.

Hence it is that the problematic of transparency cannot be isolated from the larger question of civil society. Before the collapse of the U.S.S.R., Michael Kennedy argued (1991: 1):

The principles of a civil society challenge fundamentally the organizing principles of a Soviet-type society. Where the Soviet-type system is based on the unity of state and society, civil society depends on their separation. Where the Soviet-type system acknowledges no antagonistic interests, civil society assumes them to exist and prepares rules to adjudicate among antagonists. Where the Soviet-type system is founded on the belief that a single party can rule in the interests of the whole of society, civil society assigns no group or organization that right without recurrent contest.

It can be argued now in retrospect that on the matter of civil society, the Polish party-state suffered the disadvantage of advantage. Official authority, while not as absolute and totalitarian as more fervent Western anticommunists believed, still extended deeply into every dimension of Polish life, and especially into the workplace. With the broad scope of this legitimated power came more than the usual hubris. Buried in this particular theory and practice of Soviet-style statecraft was that awesome burden feared and avoided by every Western politician--the potential to be assigned public responsibility for failure.

Hence, in Soviet-style (Laba prefers the term Leninist) societies there could *officially* be no economic crisis, there could *officially* be no educational crisis, there could *officially* be no social crisis--at least to the extent that serious questions of institutional (including party) legitimacy would be raised. Nor could there be that maddening array of moving targets so familiar to the West, which serve both to diffuse criticism and, as buffers, to deflect rage and discontent. The communist authorities could not point to opposition parties because opposition was contained within the one-party structure. They could not convincingly blame a bloated bureaucracy, as they were its makers. They could not blame greedy industrial enterprises because they ran them. They could not hold accountable Western bankers because they had made deals with them. They could not claim they were buffeted from every side by special interests and their lobbyists because these were the instruments of "bourgeois democracy." The only tactics of evasion were to be the increasingly jaded and unconvincing ones of blaming deviationists, revisionists, or reactionaries. When these tactics failed, the only recourse was the installation of a "reformist" regime. And finally, as a last resort, there was force or the threat of force, from both internal and external origins. But in the last analysis, with more or less absolute authority, there could only be more or less absolute accountability.

At first look, the question of Polish part-state transparency might appear to favor a movement such as Solidarity. But before one is tempted to find an advantage in the structural disadvantage of workers and other ordinary poles, it is important to consider the long, difficult, and perilous road to independence--a road marked by collective discovery of the roots of betrayal. The interdependent and dialectical questions of mobilization and consciousness did not emerge ex nihilo. Nor did they flow mechanistically from the wellsprings of macrostructural contradictions and state delegitimation considered in the opening chapter.

The process of defining and offering reasons for betrayal was limited by idealist and materialist factors that had to be transcended by the opposition in Poland. Though the situation of the state was one of more or less monopoly of real power, these conditions introduced only the potential for the party-state to be held accountable. The development and transformation of consciousness on the side of opposition forces had to occur despite specific opaque conditions. For example, the Polish situation did not feature antagonists clearly polarized into competing camps based on such categories as race, ethnicity, gender, or unidimensional conceptions of class. Thus, the Polish workers' struggle was not a matter of people of color rising against privileged whites. It was also not a simple movement against external domination in the sense of anticolonial struggles throughout the third world. Nor was the movement an ethnic and national revolt rooted in the denial of faith and language--as Poles had successfully retained both forms of cultural identity under centuries of external pressure. All of this is not to say that grievances were somehow not real. It is rather to say that the resistance was not advantaged from the onset by the galvanizing strength brought to a movement by the clear polarization of forces along racial or other lines.

If the mobilization of Polish workers and their allies was disadvantaged by the absence of clear and dichotomous categories of haves and have-nots, the movement was advantaged by other resources that could be brought to bear over time. The more important ones teach us once again that successful movements are seldom totally spontaneous.

1. The role of trade unions in Poland prior to Solidarity, while structurally contained by the party-state, provided specific avenues for organization. To begin, despite the fact that the old CRZZ (the federation of Polish labor) was an instrument of state planning, the union enrolled some 95 percent of the working population in the decade before the rise of *Solidarnosc*. It would be naive to confuse the numerical strength of state unions with real power. However, the ubiquity of membership could not fail but facilitate the later authentic forms of organization making that rendered *Solidarnosc* a force for change.

2. Certainly there existed no Western or U.S. style of collective bargaining for Polish workers under the old regime, but this did not mean that the state unions were always silent and passive. In the pre-*Solidarnosc* decade, the union leadership (under the official state structure) did bring pressure to bear at the ministry level on issues of wages, hours, and working conditions. At the plant level, unions as well as management were active in determining the adjustment of bonuses, workers could be removed from a job only with union

approval, and overtime was subject to union consent (Ludlow, 1975). These were issues of limited scope, as decisions of substance were to be ratified if not initiated by the State. The point to be made, however, is that when *Solidarnosc* leaders at the Gdansk shipyards negotiated their demands, the negotiation mode (as well as the will to strike in the face of brutal force) were well established in Polish industrial relations. Certainly, the specifics of those demands and the larger questions of historical context and organizational change were to prove to be radically different from the old State Union structure, which provided only the form and not the substance of worker's power.

3. Roman Laba has argued that "the rediscovery of the sit-down strike, the development of the interfactory committee and the creation of the national structure--reflect the operative dynamics of the organizing heritage that produced the independent union" (1991: 112). The first two elements demonstrate once again that *Solidarnosc* did not emerge ex nihilo. As early as 1931, sit-down strikes made their debut in Poland, and by 1933 they grew to become a distinctive tactic to redress workers' grievances.

The rise of the sit-down strike in Poland had a domino effect on workers in other countries. From May through June 1936, a massive sit-down strike movement swept across France (where it was called a Polish strike). In the United States in December of that year, the sit-down was decisively used in the strike that began in Fisher Body No. 2 in Flint, Michigan. "The Great Sit-Down," as it has been called, brought General Motors to its knees, became the model for the newborn Congress of Industrial Organizations (CIO), and hastened the unionization of most of American heavy industry over the next five years. (Laba, 1991: 102)

The power of the party-state in postwar Poland made the sit-down dangerous, and it was seldom used until the December 1970 strikes for free trade unions in Gdansk, Gdynia, and Szczecin. In January of 1971, the Warski Shipyard struck, making full use of the sit-down and forcing the state elite (including the first secretary and the premier) to negotiate with workers. In the same period of labor unrest, the state had responded to the threat to its hegemony by encouraging the formation of strike committees in the hope they could be coopted to manage discontent. However, the strike committees became interfactory in form, adding to the organizational strength of the movement. (This success contributed to the organizational foundation for the interfactory strike committee at Gdansk a decade later.)

On one level, then, the party-state as of December 1970 was already losing organizational control of the Polish workers' movement. On the other, Polish workers were demonstrating increasing tactical sophistication. They were even then building upon a history of protest that had confirmed the inextricable link between union effectiveness and organizational independence from the party and state. These lessons were, as always, learned the hard way. But they contributed to the continued emergence of a revolutionary consciousness.

4. The question of revolutionary consciousness cannot be disassociated from the formation of some historical memory. And on this level, the events of December 1970 loom large in the pre-*Solidarnosc* decade. As a Christmas gift

to Polish workers on December 12, the Gomulka regime announced sharp price increases for food and other consumer goods. Workers took to the streets in Gdansk on December 14, in Gdynia on the 15th, and in Szczecin two days later, demonstrating the collapse of official legitimacy at the plant level as well as at the center. It is not necessary to review again the escalation of street battles, the burning of party headquarters, and Gomulka's resort to tanks to put down the risings on the Baltic by brutal force. If the occupation strike and the interfactory committees were the organizational legacies of these events, the blood of martyrs fired a simmering and enduring culture of resistance. One particular photograph in Gdynia is sufficient to show how imagery captures present events yet simultaneously forms the memory that propels the future.

There is a moment in all this that a photographer with a single click of his camera will etch into the memory of the Polish people and later, through the film artistry of Andrzej Wajda, into the consciousness of people throughout the world. A door is ripped off a commuter train and used to support the body of a dead worker. Six men lift it to their shoulders and lead a surging crowd through the streets of the city. It is a stunning photograph, one that exudes the emotions of horror and massive indignation and embattled dignity that were at the heart of the coastal rising. When Wajda came to make his classic film of *Solidarnosc*, MAN OF IRON, he could, in the name of high drama, do no better than recreate with zealous attention to detail the scene fixed by the photograph. (Goodwyn, 1991: 122)

The events of late 1970-1971 did more than bring down Gomulka. They left a searing memory of betrayal, beyond the practical knowledge of how to channel outrage along tactical and organizational lines. In the early stages of the strike in Gdansk a decade later, Lech Walesa demonstrated the power of historical memory in specific terms. In addition to demands for a 2,000 zloty pay increase and the reinstatement of principal leaders, the strikers sought to raise a monument to the victims of December 1970 (Walesa, 1987: 121). The Gdansk memory meant that the events of 1970 were, in real terms, an historical dress rehearsal for the 1980 rising that shook the East and the world.

THE RELATIONAL HISTORY OF A SOCIAL MOVEMENT

With some sense of movement assets and liabilities in mind, it is now possible to delineate the *mobilization* of *Solidarnosc*, its *transformation* from a movement of narrow unionist (and quite possibly accommodationist) goals to a broadly based movement supported by peasants and intellectuals, a *credibility* phase in which the regime was forced to recognize the popular authority of the movement and bargain accordingly, and finally an *institutional* phase which marks the formal taking of state power. In this chapter, the primary focus will be on mobilization and transformation, with the latter phases considered later. However, a word of caution is in order. As history and movements do not conform to linear measurements of time and discrete construction of phases, it will be necessary to move less by chronological order than through linking conceptually aligned events not necessarily sharing a specific frame of time. Such phase events must also be more precisely linked with the preceding structure of forces in chapter 1, intended to orient initial inquiry. Thus, we shall from time to time offer an integrating summary of these more macro forces.

Anthony Oberschall delineates the mobilization of a social movement as follows:

The minimum conditions of collective protest are shared targets and objects of hostility held responsible for grievances, hardship and suffering, augmented in some cases by more deeply rooted sentiments of collective oppression, common interests and community of fate. These minimum conditions give rise, however, to only short-term, localized, ephemeral outbursts and movements of protests such as riots. For sustained resistance or protest an organizational base and continuity of leadership are also necessary. (1973: 119)

Solidarnosc was both agent and object of transformation. Beginning as the narrowly focused "trade union" so recognizable in the United States today, the movement was to grow by expanding both its grievances and its base. As a social movement in the most rudimentary sense, *Solidarnosc* was to represent the bonding together of persons intent on changing an existing aspect of social order. Through its clashes with the forces of the former Polish state, it developed and redeveloped an architecture that allowed for the systematic construction of movement strategies and tactics, ideology and policy - and the direction of collective action toward movement objectives. As a social movement, it developed over time a richly layered imagery distinguishing for its followers between reality and illusion, right and wrong, authority and illegitimate power.

We undertake this journey with a cautionary note. Roman Laba (1991: 312) has argued against elitist interpretations of history--whether found in the Leninist model of the state with its emphasis on a party vanguard or even among sympathetic voices, such as that of Leszek Kolakowski, who argue that intellectual leaders provided the architecture of the union and fashioned the ideology of Solidarity. Kolakowski held that the KOR (Committee for the Defense of Workers), while not responsible for Solidarity strikes, were very much influential in the realpolitik of grievances and demands. A harsher view of the bottoms-up phenomenon in *Izvestia* in 1985 predictably referred to the masses of workers drawn to Solidarity as lacking in class consciousness and susceptible to extremism. In both cases, the role of ordinary people is diminished.

To attribute leadership roles to an intellectual or other elite may rest more on ideology than on evidence. Noting that Polish social scientists failed in the postwar period to develop a political sociology of the working class, Laba studied the documentation kept by the Solidarity movement, which detailed demands, agreements, and historical records relating to strikes, negotiations, and ideology. He concludes that the main characteristics of solidarity, its master frames, were created autonomously by Polish workers six years before the creation of KOR and ten years before the rise of Solidarity (1991:11).

The significance of the working class as an agent of political action stands in opposition to the traditions of conservative Western social thought as well as the critical tradition of C. Wright Mills (who was wary of the "labor metaphysic" in explaining modern change). My observation may be unfair to Mills, who was documenting the rise of the white collar American workforce and the corresponding decline of the traditional blue collar. Such processes continue in the West, and particularly in the United States, until this day. However, the argument can be made that the Polish working class proved to be a much more powerful revolutionary force than its counterpart in the United States.

It should be reiterated that the mobilization and emergence of Solidarity cannot be understood by recourse to structural forms of teleology, claimed to be revealed in the laws of history. Whatever the long term, Poland and Solidarity were not and are not viewed in these pages as marching toward some preordained and final end. This movement, as others, must be understood as context bound. I have already explored the vital macrostructural milieux in which the movement was to rise. However, it must also be viewed as hanging in the balances of a turbulent present, with human beings defining, negotiating, and struggling toward a precarious future. The tendency to think in terms of a vulgar structuralism not only omits the world of human agency and psychic synergy, it also deemphasizes the specific conditions evidenced in a history of resistance.

However, if an oversocialized conception of movements is in error, so too is a destructuralized account. The view here is a relational one, in which historical structures of economy and state interact with the forces of culture and ideology at the macro level. These in turn shape the internal dynamics (organization, program, strategies, and tactics) of movements, which in their dynamic formations act back on these higher and more systemic forces. In the process, a synthesis emerges in which old forces and new, Western conceptions of markets and civil society together with Polish traditions of spiritual transcendence and social justice will clash in building and rebuilding the Polish future. No movement, and no people, escape either the past or the future.

As Michael Kennedy notes (1991:11), social movements are not timeless. Neither are they ephemeral. However, an important distinction must be drawn now between the views of the French structuralists such as Althusser and thinkers such as Lukacs on the question of consciousness. For the former, ideology and subjectivism are peripheral consequences of social structure. Laws unfold in history "independent of human will, consciousness and purpose....the *masses*, caught in the structurally determined relations of class struggle, are more the instruments than the makers of history" (Perdue, 1986: 331). For the latter, the mature thought of the proletariat "features understanding, not simply of the isolated past but the historical processes that unite eras, ideologies and destinies" (Perdue, 1986: 371).

Neither Althusser or Lukacs would be prone to find class consciousness in the theoretical Marxist sense in the Solidarity movement. Certainly this was a movement directed against the party-state apparatus of "real" Stalinist socialism, not against capitalist order. However, that the movement reflected historically founded consciousness is evidenced both in formal documentation and in what George Rude terms the "ideology of popular protest." Thus the interaction between the popular and the more formalized ideologies will both shape and reflect the strategy, tactics and symbolism of the movement.

The word "authentic" is from the Greek *authentikos* which translates roughly as "made with one's own instruments or tools." To pull together the threads of argument thus far, it is useful to conceptualize Solidarity as an authentic social movement fashioned from the specific instruments of Polish consciousness and organization. The movement can be said to have emerged in the milieux of world and regional crisis, but these conditions of higher crisis were mediated through delegitimation of the Polish party-state. The power and centrality of that institution ultimately ensured that it could not escape responsibility. However, in the years of advance and retreat, challenge and negotiation, Solidarity's leaders and legions proved adept at seizing opportunities and adapting responses to ever-changing circumstances of crisis. However, they could not invent from a world of definition and meaning the overarching systemic forces of the global market--and their collision with a Soviet second world seeking access and finding dependency. These forces were structural, and they were historical.

Just as the specific conditions of world and regional crisis were distinctive for the "East" in general and for Poland in particular, so too were the relations of power. In 1951, Rudolph Heberle included fascist and communist forms of social movements in his analysis of political sociology. However, when such movements are successful in taking the total power of the state, or (as in the case of Poland) a new elite comes to power in part with external support, the context within which future opposition movements must mobilize changes dramatically. Any attempt to analyze movement dynamics for movements such as Solidarity must recognize that altered reality.

In Poland, a new indigenous elite emerged in the postwar era, and it held power not by means of concentrated wealth but through statist control of the means of production and through the control of access to the means of influence (media and education). Although a number of democracy movements arose in the 1980s and early 1990s worldwide, Solidarity stands as an exemplar of a new force on the world stage. The official ideology of the party elite was that democracy represented a mystification and that a vanguard was essential to advance the people's interest. While it is important to avoid sweeping historical generalizations, it can be said that the rise of Solidarity in the context of a self-declared Leninist state constituted an unprecedented event. The question to be answered, however, is how did a democracy movement emerge in such an unlikely setting? More profoundly, what particular categories of Polish workers were drawn to the movement in its mobilization stage? Secondarily, what was the early ideology of Solidarity and in what ways did it bear the mark of earlier expressions of popular protest in Poland? And finally, by what alternative communication channels did the workers reach other constituencies? This is a daunting question, given the state-controlled media committed so frequently to the discreditation of Solidarity.

GDANSK: CRUCIBLE OF MOBILIZATION

For many, Solidarity was born on August 31, 1980, when a committee of strikers in Gdansk negotiated an agreement with state authorities, ensuring the right to form independent trade unions. In a formal sense, this can be considered correct. However, there are important precursors to be acknowledged. Within the generalized crisis specified above, the 1976 strikes are of specific importance for several reasons. To begin, there is a tendency to focus only on the more violent strikes at Radom and Ursus in June, which were met with brutal measures by the regime. However, during this summer of discontent, workers all over Poland engaged again in occupation or sit-down strikes inside factories. Such a tactic "required a considerable amount of organized worker cohesion" (Goodwyn, 1991: xxiii). The date of this more organized resistance is also significant. It occurred in advance of the formation of the KOR, the organization of intellectuals in Warsaw often credited with being the early ideological drivers of the movement.

A critique of the elitist thesis was mounted earlier. However, to dichotomize is to perhaps miss the larger point. KOR intellectuals put much at risk between 1976 and 1980, exploring in print the issues relating to trade unions and publishing a "Charter of Workers' Rights" (1979). In some ways KOR members were the forerunners of support for Solidarity from academics and students. Acknowledging their role does not diminish those whose strikes put them in harm's way, and may lead us to see the interplay between movement realpolitik and other resistance groups. Those who would credit KOR unduly, however, miss the larger truth: these intellectuals were putting in conceptual form a real struggle waged by those sweating for a living.

More to the point, perhaps, is an appreciation of the sophisticated organizational structure that coordinated the series of strikes on the Baltic coast that marked the turbulent coming of Solidarity in Gdansk in 1980. With its genesis in the 1970 events already considered, the Interfactory Strike Committee linked factories and cities by the score and workers by the hundreds of thousands. Headed by a strike presidium, this apparatus was able to implement concerted programs of job action and to raise the specter of a general strike. The building of the apparatus, its symbolism, and its tactics were authentic, forged in the fires of experience. However lofty (and intellectually appealing) the sphere of axiology and written demands, ideas still must be translated into action.

In a context of worsening economic conditions, and the glaring contradictions of inequality in a nominal socialist state, the regime was content to repeat its favorite tactic of political roulette, Russian style. In July of 1980, it raised food prices, giving rise to "a wave of rolling strikes that continued in various parts of the country" (Laba, 1991: 95). These were only a preview of the shape of things to come. On August 14, at six o'clock in the morning, workers in the Lenin Shipyard struck, followed by the Paris Commune Shipyard in Gdynia on the 15th and the Warski Shipyard in Szczecin on the 16th.

The fact that the mobilization of the workers' movement in 1980 began in Gdansk comes as no surprise. Given the specific history of the formation of a culture and movement of resistance, it could have occurred no where else with such force. What was to become *Solidarnosc* was driven in the early stages by a specific class fragment (shipyard workers, routinely younger and better educated) and facilitated by a distinctive regional geography (the Baltic coast) that aided communication and political contagion. By the end of that fatal year, these more specific conditions had been generalized beyond the region and beyond working people to touch the lives of Poles from different walks of life.

The immediate events surrounding the strike appeared ordinary enough, given the record of turbulence of the prior decade. Two of the official preliminary demands in the program Walesa had drawn up were no different from those emanating from earlier actions across the country: the reinstatement of leaders (in this case, Anna Walentynowicz, Andrzej Kolodziej, and Walesa) and a raise in pay of 2,000 zlotys. However, the maturation of the resistance was evidenced in two additional demands conceived by Walesa--one preliminary and open, the second to be sought only after it was clear that the members of the Free Trade Union were unified in support of a radical change in Polish industrial relations.

The third preliminary demand was mentioned earlier: the request to raise a monument to those workers slain at Gdansk in December of 1970. This demand was more than a gesture, and more than a symbol of defiance. It was a grim reminder of betrayal by the party-state. This demand set the stage for what Walesa described as the central demand: the right to autonomous trade unions that were to be structurally independent of state authorities--whether at the center or at the local plant level. Even at this fateful moment, Walesa and other leaders were not sure whether the members or their leaders were ready for such audacity. Many had already thought the unthinkable. Now they were to demand what the party-state could not surrender without abandoning all preexisting claims to legitimacy. However, by the end of August, a Soviet-style regime did the unprecedented. When the Central Committee was informed by General Jaruzelski that the Polish army would not clear occupied factories by force of arms, the regime recognized independent trade unions--and their right to strike when collective bargaining failed (Bialer, 1981: 529).

Given the regime terror that ended the 1970-1971 dress rehearsal, to have sought authentically free trade unions was a courageous and perhaps premature step. Walesa in his *Path of Hope* (1987) worried that another year or two was needed to prepare both workers and their leaders for the momentous action to come. However, as he succinctly noted in his later reflections, the leadership had been overtaken by events. So it was for the ringleaders of the Solidarity movement born during that August of discontent. The road to Gdansk had been paved by the higher forces of macrostructural and institutional failure, together with the realpolitik of party betrayal, in interaction with a movement in transition. The road from Gdansk would show a similar course of development, but that is a subject for the chapter to come. For now, it is time to complement and extend the transformation of the workers' movement from a more material level by examining the permutations of its ideology.

THE IDEOLOGY OF THE SOLIDARITY MOVEMENT

To comprehend the ideology of Solidarity requires some prior discussion of this somewhat troublesome concept. In such an attempt, the work of Karl Mannheim is instructive. In his classic *Ideology and Utopia*, Mannheim argued that politics involves more than a "struggle for power." At an ideational level, power struggles advance a "political conception of the world" (1968: 36, originally published in 1936). Beyond the issues of particular ideology (the truth value of assertions) is the larger domain of total ideology, which reflects opposing worldviews. Such thought systems can be divided into two Weberian-style ideal types: those that encapsulate the interests of the existing order and those that represent the forces of change.

For purposes of analysis, movement ideology refers herein to a system of delegitimations as well as legitimations. It follows that opposition movements (such as Solidarity) adhere to political ideals that challenge the existing institutional order while self-identifying the movement as a force for legitimate change. At the highest level of abstraction, opposition ideology embodies a political *weltanschauung*. The discourse at this level may appeal to such values as human rights, democracy, and nationalism while identifying regime and institutional authority (legitimated power) as somehow responsible for the denial of such basic rights. At a more derivative level, movement ideology will make the case for justice in concrete and specific language. With regard to the structure of thought, the constellations of discourse within the movement define different levels of grievance.

At the most rudimentary level, often in the early stages of a movement, grievances reflect a breach of faith (failure to perform). Put concretely, at this stage of popular protest it appears that the two sides share a common legitimacy base and that grievances should be resolved according to a process that does not threaten the boundaries of the existing systemic order. At a more mature stage of the movement, pending dialectic relations between the forces of institutional authority and those of the opposition, new and transcendent articles of political faith may emerge. Here, the political stakes are raised as the resolution of grievances now implies the collapse of legitimated power and the construction of new institutions. At this stage, it follows that the basis for crisis can no longer be defined as a breach of faith that can somehow be contained without altering essential power relations. Instead, the breach has been transformed into an abyss.

To chronicle the events that represent the emergence, transformation, and institutionalization of Solidarity is not sufficient. The ideological permutations of the movement have a richness that demonstrates the active formation of consciousness. In the context of a dynamic interplay with higher and immanent forces, the legitimation system for the resistance was shaped through a dialectic--between popular symbolism and ideology (often forged in industrial action and in the streets) and more formalized constructions found in movement publications and written demands. For purposes of analysis, we can trace the dialectical maturation of the ideology of Solidarity from a traditional base through levels of resistance--first to party-state incompetence and finally to a recognition of structural barriers and existing institutional contradictions.

I have already noted that linear models of change, whether encompassed in the historical development of a movement or in the consideration of its ideology, are misleading. Solidarity, as many movements, demonstrated surges and retreats in consciousness, boldness and caution in demands, heady advances and painful retreats on the road to power. However, a review of both of the popular watchwords of the movement and an analysis of the more formalized demands of a maturing movement demonstrate a maturation born of experience and popular support. In the pages to come, I will argue that the ideology of resistance, within the movement of workers and their allies, was actively shaped by participants in the context of ongoing events. However, the maturity of later phases was not to represent a repudiation of what went on before. Quite to the contrary, the ideology of *Solidarnosc* grew in complexity because of the continuing impact of older forces in Polish institutional life. Still, if the focus is narrowed to include those momentous events of late 1970 and early 1971, stretching to the Round Table of 1989, distinctions can be made that mark the cumulative maturation and the emergence of new contradictions within movement ideology.

During the initial phase, the watchwords and demands of 1970-1971 reflected a resistance informed by traditionalism and the delegitimation of the party-state apparatus. By 1980, a second ideological phase was evidenced in the elaboration of a more general value construction (centering on democracy and independence) within the movement. Such elaboration did not replace earlier ideological formations, but added to them a growing sophistication and complexity in Solidarity's political view of the world. And there is more. Second phase ideology demonstrated greater specificity in calling for new and independent organizations to achieve labor demands. This does not mean that demands for an independent union emerged with the birth of solidarity. However, the meaning of independence over the decade moved from watchword status and empty demands to a codified position rooted in the maturation of a bargaining paradigm. Such contractualization pointed the way to the critical conclusion: that the axiology of freedom and the material hopes for a better life could not be realized under the existing order. Thus, on the political side, calls for union democracy were to give way to calls for general democracy. At the time of the third and final phase, Solidarity had moved from a general movement of resistance and transformation to the party of institutional power. Although emerging in Solidarity's wilderness years between martial law and the

Round Table (see next chapter), the view of Western-style institutions was not confined to the sphere of the state and civil society. Once Solidarity gained state power, a third strong and open ideological phase saw the emergence of support for economic formations long missing from Polish national life: the construction of a Polish market economy.

The workers' ideology of resistance was in significant measure shaped by the traditional forces of nationalism and religion. Through centuries of domination by divergent powers, Poles had kept alive their language and their faith. Nationalism for most Poles also meant that there were authentic manifestations of cultural expression that represented the symbolic negation of socialist realism. Solidarity did not create this quest, but it was to later speak the language of Polish resistance by insisting on opening the painful chapter of the Katyn woods massacre and by inviting exile poet Czeslaw Milosz to read his work in Poland. Nor did Solidarity invent the latent hostility toward Russia. Still, whatever the appeal of Leninism and modernization for many Poles, the indigenous memories of imperial occupation were always close to the surface (Kennedy, 1991: 65). Solidarity was ultimately to serve as a channel for a more generalized resentment of domination .

But in the factories and on the streets in 1970-1971, Polish workers were not demanding a reopening of the Katyn woods massacre or that the works of exile poets be embraced in recognition of a Polish glasnost. In the grey and grim December of 1970, about a thousand workers marched on Gdansk in support of the shipyard strike. Among the routine slogans of "work" and "bread" was a familiar refrain: "Poland Still Lives." On December 15, a throng of perhaps 15,000 unarmed demonstrators marched on party headquarters and set it afire. Refusing orders to disperse, they suffered a volley of shot and shells from an army detachment sent to defend the building. There, with some bleeding and dying, a voice from somewhere began to sing the first line of the Polish national anthem: "Poland lives while we live." When the line, "March, March Dabrowski" was sung, the crowd moved forward, in grave danger of facing the withering fire of automatic weapons. However, those in the police and military were also Poles. They refused orders to spill Polish blood in defense of party headquarters - and left the building (Laba, 1991: 27-33).

The anthem, and the deep nationalist sentiments it inspired, were to play a particularly crucial symbolic role a decade later. In the Polish August of 1980, the state media sought to break the strike at Gdansk and leave Solidarity politically stillborn. The official line was that honest workers did not want to take part and that only malcontents were holding out. Klemens Gniech, the director of the yard, announced over the loudspeaker that the talks over the initial weekend had resulted in a "full agreement." The purpose was to divide the strikers inside from the desperately needed support of the workers outside, who were coming to work on a Monday morning.

Walesa suddenly appeared, climbing up where all could see him. ....He surveyed the crowd and then, alone, in his loud distinctive voice, began singing the national anthem, "Poland Has Not Yet Perished." The workers joined in on both sides of the gate. With a measure of solidarity to build upon, Walesa then reviewed the shipyard director's claims, refuted them briefly and moved to the central issue - the situation of all the striking workers throughout the tri-cities. The strike, he said, was for the defense of all workers of the coast and, indeed, of Poland. Turning to the throng waiting outside, he said: "Don't hesitate to come in. We have to fight for what is rightly ours. Come to us, shipyard workers. There's nothing to be afraid of." A vanguard of mostly younger workers came. ....then they all came, to prolonged cheering. (Goodwyn, 1991: 174)

There is more to Polish nationalism than anthems of resistance. Roman Laba has argued that Solidarity invoked other images of traditional symbolism, which were used to tie the movement to a messianic myth, long established in Poland, that presents the country as "bulwark of the West against Eastern barbarism" (Laba, 1991: 144). However, it was the new symbols of workers' nationalism that demonstrated the maturity of Solidarity. Solidarity created posters and badges that reminded Poles of workers' risings since Poznan of 1956 and chronicled the repetitive response of the party-state in the official watchwords of denial that met each succeeding rising. Among the more typical official labels were "hooligans," "anarchists" and "malcontents."

Laba also notes that *Solidarnosc* did not resort to dehumanizing symbols in an attempt to control political discourse. In lieu of vilification, those in the movement chose to symbolically ignore the party-state. Laba is in part correct when he notes that such tactics contributed to the moral integrity of the movement while rejecting symbolic preludes to violence (as violence itself) as noncreative. However, to his observation must be added two essential points. One is that the opposition, though becoming bereft of authority, nevertheless had recourse to massive power, including the prerogative of inviting troops from the U.S.S.R. to restore order. This doubtlessly ensured that open and official symbols of movement resistance would resort to more oblique attacks on authority. The second point is more complex. Solidarity manipulated symbols in sophisticated ways that undermined its adversary's claims to normative legitimacy.

For example, the nationalist symbolism of the movement took graphic form in the design featuring the word SOLIDARNOSC in red letters on a white background, with a flag rising from the letter N. Jerzy Janiszewski, the 29-year-old artist from Gdansk, added the flag to convey the message of a universal rising to the surging movement of red letters of social revolt on a field of white (Laba, 1991: 132-33). Also, Solidarity's posters, badges, slogans, demands, ceremonies, and publications featured symbols constructed from the ongoing crisis played out in the lives and resistance of workers, without identifying directly the source of their misery. Thus it was that in Solidarity's visual symbolism, the enemy of the people routinely had no face. But it is perhaps this very facelessness that was to be ingrained in Polish consciousness as the ultimate symbol of the party-state: omnipresent and depersonalized, its power apparently emanating from nowhere, lacking even the legitimacy offered by the false face of a paternalist figure such as Stalin.

Religion, tied to national expression, is also fundamental to Polish nationalism. The relationship between church and society cannot be reduced to the simple dichotomies of opiates and values so common to Western sociology. Religion in the history of Solidarity takes on the character of struggle, with all eyes seeing God through the prism of contending forces. Perhaps it is for this reason that the faithful reason that the atheistic party-state would by its very nature oppose the church. To argue that many Roman Catholic Poles were (and are) deeply religious is true enough. But to transform the church into an open ally of Solidarity on these premises would be to seriously miss the point. The role of the institutional church in Polish history and in the history of Solidarity must be distinguished from the role of religious faith. Though it is important to avoid absolutes, religious faith played a far more crucial role in the perseverance of Solidarity and its moral authority than did the institutional church in Poland.

In the immediate postwar era, Polish authorities conformed more or less with Stalinist principles on the repression of religion. In 1949, the Vatican declared that Catholics should be anti-Communists; not only should members of the community of faith not support the party but they should avoid reading its literature. However, after the tumult that brought Gomulka to power in 1956 came an uneasy rapprochement between church and party-state. The regime sought to capture legitimacy through liberalizing its censorship policies to the benefit of the journals published by the Catholic intelligentsia and by ceasing opposition to the teaching of the faith. The delicate balancing act required of church authorities in Poland was evidenced in their responses to both strikes and risings of the 1970s, and the events of the Polish August in 1980. On the one hand, church authorities routinely called for an end to police repression and for more humane economic policies. On the other, they counseled worker prudence. For example, in 1976, the Polish episcopate issued a call for Poles to strive for the "common good" and to work harder to "maintain order." Four years later, in the context of the strike at Gdansk, Cardinal Wyszynski delivered a sermon calling for worker moderation. He was ignored (Szkolny, 1981: 8-11).

However, one momentous event associated with the institutional church is not to be ignored because it reveals the importance of religious symbolism in Polish national resistance. As argued by M. Szkolny:

The power of this symbolism was evident in the extraordinary mass political catharsis induced by the election of Karol Wojtyla as Pope and his subsequent triumphal tour of his homeland; for several days the major cities of Poland lived in a carnival-like atmosphere. A whole generation experienced for the first time a feeling of collective power and exaltation of which they had never dreamt. The party apparatus with its omnipresent tentacles stretching into every corner of society appeared in this brief historic moment as a mere cobweb. If religion in prewar Poland was the opium of the people, it became in this moment the "heart of a heartless world." (1981: 10)

The point to be drawn from this has little to do with the timidity or temerity of the church hierarchy in Poland. Whatever might be said for institutional authority, the Polish Pope, as the Polish faith, belonged to the Polish people--and to skillful attempts by Solidarity to make religious symbols their own. This form of ideological cooperation is not to be understood through recourse to Western conceptions of contrived symbol making, driven by guile and well-paid media consultants seeking to fashion and shape the voice of the people. The Polish faith was ideologically shaped in the historical context of a struggle for political power. For many of the devout among the Polish people and among the activists in Solidarity, faith was a mandate for social justice. Solidarity took the icons and doctrines and made of them its own symbolic case for normative legitimacy in this world - not the next. Thus it was that after the successful strike at Gdansk in August of 1980, Walesa invoked the power and mysticism of the faith. He traveled to the shrine of the Black Madonna at Jasna Gora in Czestochowa. Here, at the 14th-century monastery on the Shining Mountain, he invoked her protection of Solidarity (Walesa, 1987: 5).

The legend of the Black Madonna stems from 1655, when the Swedes invaded Poland as part of a continuing campaign to control the Baltic states. They were successful in battle until they attacked the Paulist monastery at Jasna Gora. According to Polish religious legend, the defeat of Swedish forces on this hilltop in southern Poland was a miracle, due to the intervention of the sacred icon known as the Black Madonna found within the monastery. Described by one archbishop as the place wherein "beats the heart of Poland" (Walesa, 1987: 173), Jasna Gora remains a symbol of both divine intervention and secular resistance. Walesa's pilgrimage, as the many other rituals that forged a union between political resistance and faith, proved a masterstroke in the immanent struggle to control political discourse.

In the new republic of the 1990s, the church (as Solidarity itself) has come to symbolize the forces of order. Thus, the simplicity of struggle against common foes would give way to the complexities of new agendas in which former outsiders now hold political authority. For these reasons, as had been the case for prior regimes, the would-be architects of the new Polish order will be vulnerable to the forms of legitimation crisis reserved for those with real or perceived power to control events. But we should not reach beyond the grasp of events not yet chronicled. It is time to return to the ideological development of Solidarity.

In the preceding chapter, the delegitimation of the Polish party-state was chronicled in broad strokes. It follows that in the watchwords and slogans of the workers' movement, one should find a growing consciousness of the elementary breach of faith that infuses popular ideology. If the language of traditionalism formed a positive basis for unification within the movement, the popular ideology of "breach of faith" will serve the function of building a sense of negative oneness--solidarity against an external threat. Returning again to the initial phase, on December 14, 1970, the marchers who took to the streets to attack the symbolic edifice of party headquarters chanted more than the usual requests for bread. They called out, "The press is lying" (Kennedy, 1991: 35), and "Down with Gomulka." Slogans written on the walls of party headquarters denounced "paid lackeys of Moscow." When asked to choose leaders for purposes of negotiation, one spokesman responded that "we won't be electing anyone just yet because if we do you'll arrest them all." Later in the afternoon, one demonstrator took to the microphone to declare opposition to the "know-nothings ruling the country" and to "party committees running factory councils and unions! Down with the red bourgeoisie!"

In Gdynia, where the strike was also fully engaged, shipyard workers cried, "Out with the scoundrels! Enough lies!" One marcher later in the day carried a broom he said was pointing out the need for a "good cleanup." Another spoke of "an overthrowing, *at least in part*, of everything we hated" (italics added). Later, when a worker delegation in Gdynia presented its demands, chief among them was a call for ending the massive inequality in wages and rewards However, again the language is instructive. One leader noted that "in a land calling itself socialist, there cannot be large disproportions such as exist in Poland." Workers responded, "Now things would be like in China, everything equal" (Laba, 1991: 23, 25, 38-40).

Even though the risings of 1970-1971 were unprecedented in scope and in the frank expression of betrayal, it is clear from watchwords, slogans, and the written demands that Polish workers were only in the initial stages of a legitimation crisis. Their protests and their blood, as well as the formation of written demands (which were to be part of the heritage of the Polish August a decade later), were restricted by the normative boundaries of institutional and system maintenance. Although workers called for the downfall of Gomulka, this indicated a personification that fell short of articulating the higher institutional and systemic crisis. The denunciation of "lackeys," "scoundrels," "liars," and the like demonstrates rage, but again suggests that failure is a matter of faults of morality, will, and competence.

What appears arguable here is that the striking workers were using the existing normative order to fashion the standards by which betrayal was judged. Though the rhetoric of popular protest revealed some sentiments for an "overthrow," the essential sense of higher criticism was contained, probably more by long-standing political socialization than by fear. The possibility that the normative structure of the party-state was the source of betrayal appears to have played little role in the formation of a collective consciousness of resistance; even on the part of those workers who dared to reduce their demands to writing and present them to the authorities. Nowhere is this clearer than in the references to "socialism" and "Chinese egalitarianism" in worker attempts to legitimate their demands. At the beginning stages of Polish utopian ideology, natural rights assumed to be endemic to socialism were deemed to have been betrayed by an inept and immoral regime. However, popular ideology revealed little taste for taking apart an existing structural order. Just as European feudal institutions were to endure peasant risings for centuries, reaching at times to the executions of hated aristocrats and kings, so it was that the Polish party-state was to survive these momentous revolts. But from this point in time, the end was in sight.

The ties between traditionalism and delegitimation in the popular ideology of 1970-1971 were primary. The faint appearance of a new discourse on alternative values can be discerned, but the watchwords of revolt took the form of ambiguous symbols of solidarity such as calls for "democracy," "equality," and "free trade unions." Roman Laba concludes that the calls within the Lenin Shipyard for free trade unions in 1970 and 1971 were mostly political, given the context of a Leninist state (1991: 160). For example, demands that union leaders should not occupy executive roles in the party or workplace, that dues be controlled by worker locals and used to pay union officials, and that trade unions be empowered to publish an independent newspaper all illustrate Laba's point: a broader systemic consciousness among workers was emerging prior to the larger involvement of lawyers and intellectuals. Laba appears successful in refuting the claim that a professional elite was a necessary condition for the birth of Solidarity in 1980. However, it is self-evident that the 1970-1971 demands were either stillborn or subject to party-state cooptation. This implies both conceptual and organizational immaturity, self-limiting conditions that were to weaken and fall in the macrostructural context of crisis in the years to come.

To illustrate concretely, the demands of 1970 and 1971 revealed more an attack on the privileges of the midlevel and ruling elite than a mature consciousness of the systemic origins of structural inequality. It is true that Laba's quantitative analysis of written workers' demands reveals a dramatic increase between 1970 and 1980 in the specific demand to bring family subsidies to a level of parity with the privileges of the "apparats." In 1970, the worker's demands at the Lenin Shipyard called for similar forms of leveling and an end to the privileges of supply. At Szczecin, the special entitlements of party, police, and military were denounced, including everything from lower taxes to special prices in cafeterias. However, such demands appear to be more in keeping with expectations of distributive justice than with a transformatory position on systemic injustice.

This is not to indicate that the 1980 demands throughout Poland failed to address fundamental and concrete contradictions of privilege. Indeed, unequal access to goods (an end to special shops for the party and other elite), to drugs and medical care, to housing, and the identification of other inequities in vacation facilities, pensions, bribery, corruption, and so forth were addressed time and again. However, by this point in time, the demands for economic equality and authentically free trade unions had grown both in quantity and quality from the discourse of resistance in 1970.

In 1980, the demands put forward in the Lenin Shipyard made the usual calls for economic justice (payments to strikers as vacation pay, a pay increase, establishment of salary scales, cost of living, free Saturdays, etc.), and improvement of working conditions and benefits, including health services, daycare, nurseries, paid maternity leave for mothers, lowering retirement age, and increased pension benefits. Also featured were the now routine attacks on privilege (an end to hard currency stores, appointment of managers according to merit, equality in family allowances, etc.). However, the core demands were those striking at the heart of the institutional legitimacy of the Polish party-state. The first of these called for the "recognition of the Free Trade Union, independent of the Party and of employers." Of course, the call for free trade unions was not new. What was new is that this was the single non-negotiable demand and that those making it had the unprecedented organizational strength to make it credible. (For the complete text of the Gdansk Agreement negotiated in response to the twenty-one demands of Solidarity, see Oliver MacDonald, *The Polish August*, Left Bank Books, 1980.)

The call for authentically free trade unions was only one of a series symbolizing the transformation of ideology from the specific condemnation of regimes and functionary privileges to a broader consciousness of institutional crisis. Demand number two called for a "guarantee of the right to strike, and of the indemnity of strikers and their supporters." The third demand featured "freedom of expression and of publication, an end to the suppression of independent publications, and the opening up of the mass media to representatives of all political and religious persuasions." In concert with the usual language seeking the restoration of rights for workers punished for strikes in 1970 and 1976 and for university students denied the right to continue their studies, demand number four called for the "liberation of all political prisoners and an end to repression for crimes of conscience."

And of final significance, the Inter-enterprise Strike Committee (MKS) included in its demands (five and six) "access to the mass media" and "mass circulation of all information relating to the socioeconomic situation." Moreover, demand number six transcended the call for freedom in public information merely in the abstract by linking this right to the need to "relieve the country's economic crisis." The same demand called for the right of all citizens "to take part in discussions concerning economic reforms." Thus, at Gdansk during the Polish August, the first six demands can be said to constitute a redefinition of natural rights followed by fifteen "bread and butter" demands addressing wages, hours, working conditions, and "management rights" that were clearly abused under the existing order. Whereas the latter constituted clear examples of distributive justice, the former were the basis for exposing the contradictions in Soviet-style regimes. *Simply put, the six core demands could not be met within the structural and ideological parameters of the existing order.*

Natural law here refers to those norms of behavior inherent in human relations, both personal and social, driven by an innate morality that can be discerned by reason. It can be contrasted with the statutory law that is the codified product of modern states (often parliaments or legislatures in Western representative democracies) or common law, which is unwritten and based on custom, tradition, usage, and court decisions. All modern states, including prerevolutionary Poland, boast statutory and common law. However, the redefinition of natural rights implicit in the first six Solidarity demands signified a growing dysjunction between the more formal law of the party-state, and natural law. By its denial of fundamental human rights, the party-state could now be redefined as irrational by a reasonable person possessing an innate morality.

It is not credible to assess the personal consciousness expressed in psychopolitical terms of workers who were continuing the decades-long process of constructing new definitions of natural rights and natural law during the fateful days of the Polish August in 1980. Nor is it necessary to entertain at this point the philosophical problematics of such constructs. However, what is arguable is that workers had erected a scaffolding for a new and transcendent political and economic order. These demands, in the language of my explanation, prepared the way for the transition in consciousness from the concrete political awareness of legitimation crisis to a more deeply rooted comprehension of a profound and enduring systemic crisis. However, the perception of such crisis was and still is limited to isolated and relativistic conceptions of the Soviet failure. The role of global market forces in the collapse of Soviet systemic forces, was not and is not well understood in Poland (and elsewhere). In the course of the events to come, it was only to become crystal clear to a larger audience of Poles that the ethos and program of Solidarity could not coexist with the party-state.

The permutations in the ideology of change were to continue. In 1983, Aleksandra Jasinska-Kania argued that the Polish political order faced a spreading legitimation crisis that crossed traditional lines of socioeconomic status. She argued that "law and order" views calling for unquestioning obedience were breaking down, "not only due to the fact that the authorities can no longer ensure the maintenance of order and the observance of proclaimed norms, but also because *citizens cease to regard the present order as unquestionable and demand the justification of norms of the system,* in particular as education broadens their intellectual horizons and they develop cognitive abilities and skills in participating in discourse" (1983:162, italics added.) Jasinska-Kania thus discerned a crucial shift in the post-1980 political discourse sweeping Polish society. Increasingly, terms like "social contract" and "agreement" confirmed a Habermas style of "postconventional orientation" whereby those holding the power of the state as well as opposition forces come to be judged in terms of their ability to carry out the terms of agreements in accordance with procedural rules.

Habermas and Kohlberg have compared the contractual orientation to the official morality of the American state and its Constitution. However, for Habermas, the contractual stage does not constitute an end in itself but instead prepares the way for a new transition to social democratic ideals found in the "seventh stage of universal ethics of speech" (Jasinska-Kania, 1983: 163). As noted in our earlier critique, U.S. contractualism leaves in place fundamental and asymmetrical power relations founded in questions of capital ownership and control. Such problems are now unfolding in the republic of Poland, assuming the form of a new legitimation crisis. However, the recognition of the limitations of contractualism is crucial to the makers of the Polish future.

While the debate over stages or typologies of moral orientation and rational legal authority is captivating, two crucial points must be made. First of all, the embracing of contractualism by Solidarity in Poland signified far more than a general skepticism of authority. This is because the diffusion of legalistic conceptions of authority routinely takes place within the context of a pluralistic model of society founded in competing interest groups. On the one side, pluralistic politics features movements with the organizational strength and popular support to successfully pressure central power. On the other, the center is assumed to respond in good faith to such expressions through entering into one or a number of negotiation channels whereby new laws, policies or programs are called into being. To the extent that this developed in Poland, such a conception of politics as a negotiated expression of the popular will constituted a repudiation of the vanguard ideal inherent in the Leninist conception of the party-state. It is, implicitly if not explicitly, an embracing of the ideology and formations dismissed in official party circles as bourgeois democracy.

The second point is more general and historical. Western European and U.S. conceptions of contractualism as embodied in constitutional rights have emerged historically in the larger context of a debate over market relations. The significance of the contractual debate in Poland in the early 1980s was in the creation of new grounds for political critique and action, without discernible debate over transformed relations of production. However, though the party managerial elite were to be the focus of post-Gdansk Solidarity discourse, the enlarged debate virtually assured that certain of the roots of the socioeconomic crisis would be explored. This did not mean that a transition to capitalism emerged as a topic of opposition discourse. Quite to the contrary, Polish contractualism differed historically from that of the West in that it did not follow the rise of an internal bourgeoisie; it preceded it.

All of this is not to imply that the ideals of contractualism directly produced a new market ideology and new market formations in Poland. The larger systemic collapse of the COMECON economies transcended politics, contractual or otherwise. Stated simply, the new normative structures of contractual authority in Poland introduced a higher standard of accountability. The embodiment of that political ethic within the Solidarity movement legitimated the movement as the caretaker of new conceptions of political liberty. It was thus poised to take state power with the collapse of the party-state.

POLITICAL PSYCHOLOGY AND THE POLISH TRANSITION

To this point, little has been said about the smaller-scale psychological and cultural dimensions of Polish political life, the more intimate side of the ideological dialectic. The focus on Solidarity and the Polish party-state, on the universities and the factories, on macroeconomics and movements, on structure and ideology does not expose the human face of those involved in the Polish saga. While explanations drawn from the world of higher social forces need no apology, what should be remembered is that such forces are played out in the lives of ordinary people. A brief consideration of the human side is in order, but we begin with a brief caveat.

The tendency to romanticize a culture of resistance is part of the new thought-world that followed the seachange in recent Polish life. Yet, the nuances of opposition are overlooked in the portrait of a "David and Goliath" image of mortal struggle. As we have seen, there are plentiful examples of brutal repression, which gave rise to mass opposition on the part of workers, students, peasants, and intellectuals. However, as Wedel notes (1992: 2), party "policies and prerogatives were less often obeyed or confronted [in the Soviet period] than they were circumvented, supplemented, reinterpreted, or simply explained away." Thus, rather than focus only on the drama of domination and resistance, it is necessary to broaden one's view--to discover the ways in which tactics of survival were developed. For it is possible that these tactics will find their place in the new order, especially during the long and painful process of institution building.

For example, day-to-day survival in Poland was contingent in large part on the formation of intimate social skills based on intricate personal networks. Ironically, one way to deal with impersonal bureaucracies and their categorical rules and policies was to develop relationships so that bureaucrats were no longer faceless. One method to overcome shortages was to develop informal lines of communication on where goods might be available, inside or outside official distribution systems. Thus, the Western obsession with "knowing somebody" became in Poland "knowing (almost) everybody."

The forms of more personalized social relations in the impersonal context of bureaucratic life often assumed their shape inside the traditional social circle (*srodowisko*). The circle may consist of two dozen or so intimates in a small community, or in urban areas, a much larger secondary group linked by common interests, needs, and some degree of social contact. The social circles offer mutual support but also a network that functions as a parallel structure of social order when official circles and institutions are inefficient, unreliable, or, as in some instances, repressive. Under the old order, the circle was the source of alternative information when the official truth of the media was suspect, mutual aid during periods of hardship, and shared confidence in a context of uncertainty (Wedel, 1992: 12-13). The political significance of the circles under the old order also resided in the informal reproduction of societal opposition. The organization of Solidarity on the Baltic coast was driven informally by these circles (Latoszek, cited in Kennedy, 1991: 170).

Historically then, Poles for most of two centuries experienced a dysjunction between their own culture and identity and that put in place through outside domination. Thus, the *srodowiska* were not a specific response to Soviet and party influence only, but it is arguable that these more recent outside and inside influences brought a degree of bureaucratization, cultural penetration, and ideology to bear in a highly formalized fashion. It is therefore ironic (and in some Polish circles inflammatory) to note that in this highly unanticipated way having little to do with authentic institutional autonomy, the Polish experiment in imposed statism developed its own human face by forcing the cultivation of interpersonal networks.

It is possible however, that these highly personal relationships, blended with other forces of egalitarianism that render most Poles suspicious of vast U.S.-style inequality, may be retained in the new Polish order. Also to the point, new Polish institutions in the post-Solidarity era will not resolve new forms of legitimation crisis through Western methods of mass media communication. The political and other elite must penetrate the much more formidable and skeptical truth testing of the myriad of social circles that constitute the informal organization of Polish society.

It is crucial to note, then, that the legitimacy of this movement of opposition took root in the myriad of circles that reproduced everyday social life among the great collectives of Polish social life: the workers, the peasants, and the intelligentsia. The state media, both Soviet and Polish, portrayed and constructed the official view of a "regressive" Solidarity. However, the social circles were busy in their own deconstruction of the official view. While it is true that suspicion may lead to the substitution of unsubstantiated rumor for any official view, during the formation of Solidarity, it was the messages of resistance that rang true in the ordinary social circles--despite ongoing attempts to discredit them by the official media.

There is also a social psychological aspect to this transformation of public ideology. The daunting step of breaking with delegitimated authority was a consequence of higher structural and ideological forces played out against a background of historical domination. Yet, in the psychic world, resistance took the form of deeply felt reactions of betrayal. Broken promises were not confined to the material arena. Official dogma had promised the end of alienation but delivered a world of roles and masks, barriers and walls, a division between the world outside and the world within. Solidarity, through word and symbol, introduced into the public arena a quality of life that had been largely restricted to the private sphere. Through its open defiance, the movement shattered the social masks worn to disguise a divided self (Laba, 1991: 132).

Finally, in a context of planned human obsolescence and vulnerability, in a worker's world fraught with contradiction and betrayal, the numerically and ideologically central proletariat was to rise. But this class did not rise alone. The attempt to identify the true source of power behind Solidarity obscures more than it reveals. Solidarity was a trade union movement, but it was more than this, because it appealed in Gramscian fashion to others among the disaffected in Polish society. On the side of political culture, workers, peasants, and intellectuals were united by a nationalism born of historical domination and internal betrayal. On the intimate side of everyday life, they were brought together by a shattering of masks. But, as we shall see in the chapter to come, the unity of change may break asunder under the very different conditions of a new institutional order.

Chapter 3

The Round Table and Beyond: Markets, Democracy, and a New Legitimation Crisis

The Polish August of 1980 stands in retrospect as a great divide in Eastern European history--with Gdansk as an intersection in time connecting past and future, recollection and vision, memory and the ideology of coming transformation. If the road to Gdansk was marked by high political drama commanding a world media audience, then the road from Gdansk was slower, more tortuous, and routinely forgotten by foreigners obsessed with charisma and turbulence. If the first road was traveled by those struggling with concrete questions of distributive justice, the second was the way of those confronting the more daunting issues of authentic independence and the actual taking of state power. If the first path was fraught with obstacles that challenged the valor of the opposition, the second was long and not yet traveled, trying the endurance of the human spirit. If the first road marked the transition from recurring revolt to legitimation crisis, the second led from the critique of authority to the negation of the Polish experiment with the Soviet system. The decade of the 1980s began politically in August with a successful strike spearheaded by a fledgling movement of shipyard workers led by an electrician. The decade of the 1990s began politically in the Polish December when the movement, having become a party sharing the power of the state, saw its leader freely elected as president of the new republic of Poland.

The path from social movement to institutional power cannot be traced to a single defining moment in time. However, certainly one of the precipitating events that contributed greatly to the organizational momentum and endurance of Solidarity occurred in Gdansk--with the formation of the aforementioned Inter-enterprise Strike Committee (MKS) in mid-August of 1980. As Walesa noted (1987: 128): "The government recognized the MKS's significance at once, threatening to end the shipyard strike by force once it heard of the committee's existence. The government did not want to acknowledge the legitimacy of an independent strike committee that might eventually speak for the majority of Poland's work force." The clumsy attempts on the part of officials to negotiate with non-MKS strikers failed, but it remains revealing nevertheless. It is arguable that those in beleaguered positions of authority often respond to crisis by denying both its institutional roots and the popular scope of disaffection. To focus narrowly, or to demonize "malcontents" (symbolized by MKS in this case) is more than an intellectual problem of explanatory reductionism--it is also an ideological problem of historical evasion.

However, MKS could not be localized and isolated. On the organizational side, it presented the mechanism for a unified front, cutting across the lines of division inherent in the bureaucratic organization of the shipyard workers into specialized workshops. From MKS deliberations, contentious as they may have been, came the twenty-one demands around which an increasingly sophisticated and audacious ideology of societal transformation was to be constructed in the coming months. Of course, these demands were not invented on the spot by this or any other committee. They represented the collective memory and the specific historical recollections born of earlier episodes in the Polish workers' struggle. This collision of past, present, and hope was the context within which the new deputy premier, Mieczyslaw Jagielski, arrived on August 22 to negotiate with the Inter-enterprise Strike Committee.

Tactically, the workers concentrated on their key demand: independent trade unions (Bialer, 1981: 528). The strategic significance of this demand was discussed in the previous chapter. It bears only brief repetition here. The insistence on independent unions signified that workers could not rely on the official authority and existing institutions of a nominal workers' state to defend their interests--no matter what the identity or personal appeal of new official leaders. The criticism had thus transcended personalities to become instead an indictment of structural roles. A vital secondary demand encountered strong official opposition: the workers' insistence that political prisoners be freed. Again, some interpretation is in order. It is arguable that from the perspective of the party-state that more "abstract" demands about independent unions and other questions of human rights could be finessed or suppressed later, by means of the bureaucratic and other forms of organizational advantage held by the party-state. However, the ability of that apparatus to retain power resided to some extent in its ability to punish real people in concrete ways. Winning concessions on rights is meaningless if people who lead on such issues can be punished and neutralized. However, after a final furious round of negotiations, Jagielski agreed to sign a statement promising that "no one will be punished for taking part in or aiding the strike" (Goodwyn, 1991: 253).

When at the end of the Polish August Walesa addressed the delegates to the MKS assembled in the shipyard, he declared: "We have won the right to strike, we have received guarantees of certain civil liberties and, most importantly, we have won the right to an independent trade union. All working people are now able, voluntarily, to form their own unions. They have the right to create independent and self-governing unions" (cited in Goodwyn, 1991: 253). More precisely, however, what Solidarity had successfully bargained was the right of workers to form unions that would coexist with those workers' organizations officially sanctioned by the party-state, and to strike when other means of bargaining failed (Bialer, 1981: 529). Although these concessions were unprecedented for a Soviet client regime, what the Gdansk workers had realized was only some measure of official legitimacy for their struggle. Opposition forces have often won the faint praise of recognition. The more important capacity to set and achieve demands would rest with the organizational and ideological maturity of Solidarity and its ability to form cross-stratum alliances. The victory achieved by the Gdansk strikers, historic and captivating as it may have been, was an opportunity only. And if the cost of that opportunity was high, the pain of the coming decade would be higher still.

INTERSTRATUM ALLIANCES

The legitimation of the fledgling Solidarity movement rose in concert with the collapse of the Gierek regime as the embattled party leader resigned, to be replaced by Stanislaw Kania. In the context of this political anomie, Solidarity became more than an instrument of Baltic workers and more than a vehicle for the general expression of working class disaffection. In the wake of the Polish August, Solidarity grew as a movement of opposition through forming alliances across Polish society, drawing more supporters and sympathizers in particular from a broad range of intellectuals and professional workers.

In the opening chapter, passing reference was made to the various forms of elitism directed toward the fledgling workers' movement by hard-liners within the party, among others. The official myth that Solidarity was the creation of dissident intellectuals had taken concrete form during the Polish August. Bogdan Borusewicz, a leader of the Committee for the Defense of Workers (KOR), was labeled by the authorities for "radicalizing the workers' demands" (Walesa, 1987: 129). To his credit, Borusewicz arranged for loudspeakers to broadcast reports of Politboro debate on the strike to the workers in the yard. While some Politboro members acknowledged that the strikers had legitimate grievances, others denounced the movement in terms contemptuous of workers in general. Their words would haunt them in the end, as they represented the hypocrisy of elitism in a self-styled workers' state.

Though intellectuals did not create or lead Solidarity, they played crucial consultative roles. Indeed, one of the strengths of the movement from the start was its ability to build a broad coalition of forces. On the one hand, this contributed to a wide spectrum of popular support. On the other, it ensured that the movement would gain from a diverse infusion of expertise. One of the most visible forms of support came from KOR (later renamed the Committee for the Self-Defense of Society, or KSS-KOR). As noted earlier, KOR was founded in Warsaw in 1976 by intellectuals who raised funds and offered other forms of support to workers who were victimized for their opposition. The number of formal members was small, given the audacity of the committee's agenda. However, around its core coalesced hundreds of activists and other groups advocating a diverse agenda for justice. These included the

Peasants' Trade Unions, the Free Trade Union of the Baltic, Student Solidarity
Support Committees, and several dozen unofficial bulletins, journals and book-
publishing ventures. Supported by the Catholic Church, KSS-KOR succeeded in
creating a broad front for human rights. Other opposition groups soon
emerged: the Movement for Defense of Human Rights (ROPCIO), the "Flying
University," the Confederation for Independent Poland, and Young Poland. (Laba,
1991: 94)

Before the Gdansk rising and the birth of Solidarity, KOR had already founded
Robotnik in 1979 and published its Charter for Human Rights. Thus, the role
of the intelligentsia in the movement was to prove most vital in the sphere of
mass communication. Through publications and by means of a university
underground, workers and citizens were provided with views of coastal events
that were not subject to the official filters of the state media. Communication
was the key to neutralizing one of the most successful of institutional tactics
employed against dissidents and popular movements: the artificial localization
of issues, grievances, and opposition through their separation from larger
institutional and systemic forces.

Among the KOR members present during the Polish August were Ewa
Milewicz and Konrad Bielinski, who assisted in the preparation of the strike
notice that bore the heading "Solidarity." Andrzej Gwiazda was joined by the
aforementioned Bogdan Borusewicz, as a founding member of the Committee of
Free Trade Unions on the Baltic coast. Among the biographies prepared for
Solidarity's 1981 Congress, Gwiazda was cited as a member of the
intelligentsia who had suffered politically while pursuing advanced studies at
Gdansk Polytechnic. Borusewicz was also described as from a family both
intelligentsia and worker. Another "man of letters," Lech Badkowski, was a
member of the strike presidium. About midnight of August 22, 1980, the
dissident intellectuals Tadeusz Mazowiecki and Bronislaw Geremek joined the
strikers (Ash, 1991a: 49-50).

One of the most influential of the intellectual dissidents was Bronislaw
Geremek; a member of the Polish Academy of Sciences with no contractual
right to teach the students of the University of Warsaw. Though not a member
of KOR, he was a leader of fund-raising activities on behalf of those workers
singled out for official repression during 1976. He was also a prominent
supporter of the Flying University, and his activities brought him under state
suspicion with subsequent detentions, interrogations, and searches of his home
(Goodwyn, 1991: 251). Mazowiecki became a global figure in 1989 when he
was chosen as Solidarity's successful candidate for prime minister and the first
non-Communist to lead a government in the East bloc.

The point of this brief overview is not to identify prominent intellectuals but
to argue the point that some members of the Polish intelligentsia were more
than willing to serve in a worker-led movement. If there was a tacit
requirement, it was mutual respect. However, beyond the complex mythology
of the necessity of intellectual command, and the assumption of workers'
organizational and ideological deficiencies on which that mythology rests, is a
second fable. Stated simply, it is that intellectuals (and a larger cast of
professionals) cannot, and in the case of Solidarity, did not enter into productive

alliances with those who sell their labor. Toward the aim of falsifying that myth, Ash has argued:

The first point about KOR was not that it was an initiative of Warsaw intellectuals. The first point about KOR was that it was an initiative of the intelligentsia-based democratic opposition which set out specifically to support and work with workers, and subsequently with other social groups. In any case the most notable feature of Solidarity was not that it was a mass workers' movement. The most notable feature of Solidarity was that it was a movement in which workers and intellectuals worked together, at best combining peaceful, dignified mass mobilization and skillful high-level negotiation to try to change their country. No less than half the delegates to Solidarity's 1981 congress had completed higher education. (Ash, 1991a: 50)

To comprehend the role of the intelligentsia in the broader stream of Solidarity as a social movement requires a brief foray into both history and deconstruction. Following Foucault's post-structuralism, it is not sufficient to interpret power purely in terms of state and other forms of organizational/institutional force. Although intellectuals have never reigned in the functionalist sense of Plato's philosopher-king, their constructions of truth may serve to either question or legitimate existing structures. Perhaps of greater significance than the positions taken by intellectuals is their selective silence on issues that define order and change.

In considering the relations between power and knowledge in Poland, Baranczak's distinction between the *intelektualista* and the *intelligent* is particularly on target (Kennedy, 1991: 240). The latter type holds certain of the credentials of the intelligentsia, specifically higher education and membership in a professional community of degreed persons. However, the *intelligent* refers to a narrowly trained social category, structurally integrated into an inherently regressive institutional order. For these, the imperatives of professional work and life are instrumental in nature, with the objectives of such action exogenous by nature. Conversely, the *intelektualista* is a category defined in terms of a larger sphere of societal responsibility. The distinction being drawn is not the simple dichotomy of scientist/technician or academician/pragmatist. The difference turns on a quality of mind that recognizes (or fails to recognize) the multidimensional properties of knowledge, as well as its inherently political and moral nature.

It is important not to simply transfer reasonably accurate conceptions of intellectuals (especially social scientists) in the Stalinist U.S.S.R. to Poland. Under Stalinism, Soviet social science was heavily ideologized to serve the interests of the regime. In the name of praxis, social inquiry became often little more than a crude exercise in the academic legitimation of power. The Polish situation was more complex. Historically, Polish men and women of ideas were also required to be people of ideals. Those ideals were not merely the static consequence of a cultural legacy of language, custom, and culture. The long history of external intervention and domination introduced clear and present threats to the nation and identity, threatening to marginalize or co-opt indigenous intellectuals. However, the reach of Moscow into Eastern Europe was constrained both by practical limits and by lingering indigenous resentment toward both the appearance and the substance of external domination.

In the dynamic crucible of conflict, Polish intellectuals were compelled to play two roles. On the one hand, they were the caretakers of the Polish national consciousness. On the other, as the Soviet-style state had no place for the institutions of civil society, intellectuals were compelled to negotiate an often precarious position between independence and fear. The resulting synthesis conforms to something of a Weberian ideal type--a tacit bargain between power and those expected to question the moral basis of truth. Intellectuals were free to keep alive the ideals of the Polish nation. They were also free to explore a range of theoretical ideas, even those with implications for a critique of domination. They were not free to directly and concretely criticize the regime. If intellectuals and their truths were to matter, they were compelled to work with and around the reach of state power. The Solidarity movement changed these arrangements of negotiated self-censorship. The generalized respect for intellectuals meant that they would be listened to. The struggle, first by workers and then by a multilayered movement, ensured that intellectuals (now emboldened by support, organization, and the promise of change) would have something to say and a broader platform to speak from.

Conversely, it can be argued that the higher strata intelligentsia under communism had lost status in Poland due to two specific factors. First, perhaps as many as one half of this elite stratum were killed or died in the Second World War and its aftermath. Many others fled as refugees. Secondly, given this brain drain and the predilection of the Polish communist party to prepare technicians to implement regime planning, measures were taken to replenish the educated labor force. Programs became more specialized, allowing for a narrowing of focus and the reduction of time required to take degrees. Evening schools were developed, and universities as well as secondary occupational schools increased in number and enrollment size.

Although Kennedy (1991: 239-41) repeats the common observation that these forces predisposed the traditional *intelektualista* toward revolutionary activity, a complementary argument is also supported by the evidence. Whatever may be said for the value of a broader view and more rigorous training, it is also true that the party's policies served to demystify and legitimate educational credentials. A number of Poles from the ordinary working and peasant strata of society became first-generation members of that social category able to define the relation between truth and political authority. This factor alone would appear to diminish the social distance between the traditional intellectual class and those who sweat for a living. Hence it can be argued that the predisposition to define intellectuals as irrelevant or academics as ivory tower figures removed from ordinary life would not plague Solidarity. Thus it would be that cross-stratum alliances would be facilitated by a second factor: that of intergenerational mobility ensuring the greater democratization (and credibility) of the Polish intelligentsia.

To this point, the term "intelligentsia" has been used rather loosely to include the traditional intellectuals (such as university professors, writers and artists of stature, etc.) and a professional or technical stratum. However remarkable the ties between people of labor and people of ideas, cross-class alliances were not restricted to this dyad only. As W. Adamski (Kennedy, 1991: 99) has demonstrated, the promise of Solidarity was evidenced by its appeal to the broadest range of Polish occupations. Almost 9 out of 10 skilled workers in heavy industry, and three out of four in light industry had joined Solidarity by the fateful close of 1981. Almost 7 in 10 doctors and those with higher education--along with parallel numbers of foremen, technicians, middle-level personnel, and other skilled and semiskilled workers--also joined Solidarity trade unions and aligned themselves with the movement. Six in 10 nurses, and more than 1 in 2 agricultural workers, peasant-workers, bureaucrats and administrators, higher cadre specialists, and engineers also became members. The single notable group not to exceed a majority of membership in Adamski's survey consisted of teachers; 47.5 percent joined the new union. Kennedy is probably correct in arguing that the ideological centrality of those in this profession ensured a great deal more oversight by the authorities and hence a higher degree of dependency in power relations.

The dependency thesis can be extended to other categories with a nominal majority of members. Peasants and other agricultural workers would appear to have been independent by virtue of their more or less successful resistance to collective agriculture. However, private operators are by the same token often suspicious of collective forms of opposition--especially if urban and factory based. Small landholders in Poland were also heavily dependent on the subsidies and market access controlled by the authorities in a command economy. Parallel dependency arguments can be made with regard to the other more nominally involved groups.

The mass appeal of the union *qua* social movement reflected a solidarity born of the macro and micro factors detailed in earlier chapters. However, a solidarity of resistance is founded on other more positive forms of attraction and promise. On the one side, the courage and audacity of the strikers at Gdansk had electrified the nation. It is one thing to seethe in discontent; it is quite another to withhold labor and force authorities to recognize independent unions. On the other side, the very structure of the union served to attract divergent occupations. In crucial ways, Solidarity was decentralized at an organizational level, allowing those from different occupations to anticipate a substantial measure of self-rule under union democracy. The umbrella structure of this movement (as many others) is useful in the building of coalitions of resistance at the emergence and maintenance stages. However, upon the seizure of power, fundamental divisions on questions of legitimate rule could be expected to reappear.

It would also be simplistic to argue that the Solidarity movement built the neophyte formations of civil society ex nihilo. Fundamental organizational forms existed, at least in skeletal and shadow forms, prior to August of 1980. As already noted, the church, though routinely reluctant to risk sacred authority through political opposition, was a repository of Polish nationalism and the source of sacred legitimation for Solidarity. Official trade unions, weak and puppetlike though they were, existed both as a means of diverting dissent and as an acknowledgment that some organ for workers was essential. And finally, the Polish family was routinely bonded by faith and by the material necessity of two incomes. However, these "alternatives" to political order offered neither the substance nor the appearance of consent and control to ordinary Poles. It was Solidarity that was to redefine, reorganize, and change the relations between the intimate formations of Polish life on the civil side and the coercive state on the political side. The church, whatever the public posture of its leaders, also found that its symbols could not remain somehow neutral in a struggle pitting believers against official secularists.

POLISH CIVIL RELIGION

It is arguable that the sacred tenets of Polish Catholicism joined other more secular conceptions of social justice to form a variety of civil religion. Civil religion is explored in both *Du Contrat Social* (1762) by Jean-Jacques Rousseau and *The Elementary Forms of the Religious Life* by Emile Durkheim (1912). Borrowing from their insights and refitting them for the present analysis, I will argue that civil religion designates the symbols, ideals, and institutions that legitimate a real or alternative social system. When such an idea system enters the psychic structure of the masses, it serves to mobilize a community or movement to work toward a shared vision of new political order--founded in new and transcendent civil or human rights. It is often the case, especially in industrial societies, that more secularized or "profane" values of distributive material justice, nationalism, or national liberation drive political communities. However, the case of Polish civil religion as embodied in the legitimations of the Solidarity movement, does not lend itself to a simple dichotomy of secular and sacred.

As argued earlier, the Polish Catholic church was a keeper of the nationalist flame. In the history of more secularized industrial societies, there may be little "religion" in what is called civil religion. This is not the Polish case. The liturgy of the church is rooted in national history and prose. Goodwyn (1991: 318) cites a Polish sociologist (who seldom went to Mass) explaining why he required that his six-year-old attend regularly: "If my son did not receive exposure to the Church, there isn't a single Polish poem he'd ever understand." All of this is not to romanticize the historical relation between the Polish Catholic Church and power. For many generations prior to the Second World War, the episcopate demonstrated a loyalty to the institution and a callousness to parishioners that often served to distance the church from the lives of ordinary people. In the preindustrial era, large landowners, the nobility, and the institutional church formed an aloof troika. In this century religious leaders were largely silent when striking miners were repressed in 1931 and sided with the landowning elite in 1937 when peasants struck for justice and bread. Though placed under house arrest in the early 1950s for insisting on the independence of the church, Cardinal Wyszynski later offered qualified support for both the Gomulka and Gierek regimes (Goodwyn, 1991: 317).

Still, it is arguable, though ironic, that the often contentious relations between church and the party-state in postwar Poland transformed a feudal and aristocratic religious institution. Whatever may be said for the failure of "real socialism" in Poland, the transformation of Polish class relations brought the negation of concentrated wealth, destroying the link between wealth and power. The new institutions of secular power and authority were founded on the rule of the party. Under such rule, the church was deprived of its traditional well-off patrons and faced an order in which its ideals were officially viewed as an anachronistic opiate. Such realities compelled the Church to rediscover and cautiously advance the more humanistic imperatives of its social gospel. This internal transformation is marked by several institutional events and one remarkable episode of martyrdom. That Poland offered a greater measure of religious tolerance to Jews for centuries prior to the holocaust is true enough, though it would be naive to exonerate the Catholic church from episodic expressions of anti-Judaism, which were quite logically consistent with the darker side of religious nationalism. (August Cardinal Hlond, for one, an official who died in 1948, was cast in the often intolerant mold of Pope Pius XII.) However, it was the Catholic University of Lublin, in the context of Gomulka's purge of Jewish members of the party, that provided refuge and employment for a number of the victims of official anti-Semitism. Although Cardinal Wyszynski had supported Gomulka's regime in the 1950s, he condemned the government for the coastal massacre of 1970 and its resort to brutal force at Radom and Ursus in 1976. He also gave an open defense of professors associated with the Flying University in 1978. Wyszynski's successor during the martial-law era was made of lesser stuff. Cardinal Jozef Glemp was determined to restore the institutional church to the good graces of the rulers of the Polish state. In one of his most symbolic of deeds, he removed the arch reformer and defender of workers' rights, Father Nowak, from his parish in Ursus.

However, just as the Polish faith could not be reduced to the policy and pronouncements of the episcopate, so it was that Polish priests were often prone to reject the role of servants of power. It was in the lives of the less auspicious priests that Solidarity worked its own brand of secular miracle. Throughout Poland, especially in the dark days of martial law, the printing capacity and mimeographs used to produce the announcements of the church were often used to print the bulletins, newspapers and journals of the resistance. Thus it was within the sacred quarters of the emerging Polish civil religion that priests came to find God in the faces of men and women of iron. They included such as Tischner of Krakow, Malkowski of Warsaw, Nowak of Ursus, and Bishop Tokarczuk of Przemysl. But looming above them all was the figure of Popieluszko, known affectionately as Father Jerzy. When the security police stopped his car at the darkest moment of the wilderness years, the movement gained a martyr who symbolized the transformation of the church from bystander to spiritual defender of a movement rooted in the affairs of this world.

Father Jerzy was tortured and his body thrown into the water at the Vistula dam at Wloclawek. Over 300,000 persons came to the funeral at St. Stanislaw Kostka in Warsaw, and the streets were alive with *Solidarnosc* banners (Goodwyn, 1991: 316-319.)

Thus we have an overview of the social construction of Polish civil religion in the Solidarity era. If its tenets are to be more concretely specified, they would appear to include (1) the general ideals of the Catholic tradition, which tend to place the common good and the community of faith above the market-centered individualism and achievement motivation of the U.S. civil religion; (2) the specific ideals of Polish Catholicism that feature both antifanaticism and deep faith, together with a suspicion of clerical authority especially on the part of peasants and the intelligentsia; (3) symbolic events from national history, often featuring themes of resistance such as the legend of the Black Madonna and the exploits of General Tadeusz Kosciuszko (known in the United States for services to the colonial army and George Washington) and Marshall Jozef Pilsudski (see chapter 1); (4) literary and artistic themes of national salvation such as those in the poetry of Adam Mickiewicz; and (5) secular themes of egalitarianism, reinforced by historical suspicion of the institutional elite and concentrated wealth.

As a central component of the emerging Polish civil society, the trade union was to become the embodiment of its civil religion and ultimately a guarantor of higher rights, defined and redefined by Poles as anterior to the legitimate reach of the state. Whereas official unions represented the attempt by the Polish state to foil the creation of civil society, Solidarity revealed that process to be a contradiction whose time had past. The struggle to ultimately build authentic institutions of civil society mandated a fateful alliance--one that synthesized the practical, everyday experiences of Polish workers, often expressed in popular ideology, and the more formalized and far-reaching utopia of the intelligentsia inspired to action. Before putting aside the question of trans-status unity and cooperation so crucial for the strength and endurance of the Solidarity movement, an important caveat is in order. Notwithstanding the widespread aversion to the regime and the thinly veiled derision of its failed efforts to build "real socialism"--and despite the construction of a movement ideology informed by both the Polish civil religion and the broad value outline of an alternative future--there were hidden but real structural and ideological fissures in Solidarity. The drama and courage of the movement, along with the sympathies of Western academics and observers, formed an image far too homogeneous to be accurate. Throughout its mobilization and resistance, the potential cleavages in the movement would be buried from public view, as members sought the united front of symbols and actions designed to change and ultimately bring down the existing order. However, as we shall see at a later point, the real fissures in Solidarity would be exposed only after the movement reached its institutional phase--that is, after it was successful in taking state power.

It is one thing to construct an alliance of resistance; it is quite another thing to construct the formations of coalition policy. For now, suffice it to say that

Solidarity encompassed two principal aims: social justice and the interdependent questions of altered political order. These, then, are the questions of civil society and the state. After taking the power of the state, yet another overriding imperative would surface, an imperative often passed over in the official discourse throughout the life of the Solidarity movement.

The decade of the 1980s began with the Soviet system of command economies in place. It ended with that system in shambles. The new leaders of Poland would inherit an economic order in chaos and be challenged to construct postsocialist relations between the state and a number of heterogeneous constellations of social interest. One such category was to consist of external capital and new Polish entrepreneurs. A second would be traditionalists seeking political legitimation for the moral authority of the Catholic church. A third social category would include those for whom Solidarity represented an instrument of greater egalitarianism. Each of these categories would be represented by strong intellectual and political voices, but all would speak without the benefit of institutional or human memory of Polish democracy or markets.

Stated forthrightly, the moral imperatives of the church were destined to collide with the more secularized values of Poles on issues ranging from religious education to the reproductive rights of women; even as the philosophical and technical problems associated with the legitimation and construction of a market economy were fated to collide with Solidarity's commitment to social justice. This joint structural and ideological dilemma would come to comprise a new Polish legitimation crisis in the final decade of the twentieth century: a crisis symbolized by, but not limited to, the fractioning of Solidarity as a political force. But to entertain at this point these great currents of Polish change would put us ahead of ourselves.

FROM INDEPENDENT UNION TO TRANSFORMATION

Hence, within a year of the Polish August, it was clear that Solidarity had captured the hearts and imagination of Poles and had embarked upon a course of ideological and organizational transition. The trans-status composition of the union was striking; and it is safe to argue that many Poles who were more directly dependent on the party (and thus fearful of formal affiliation) were nevertheless sympathetic to the resistance. In a fateful hour fraught with collateral political hazard for the regime, Polish peasants had also won official recognition in May of 1981.

What emerged during the sixteen months of coexistence between the party and Solidarity can be likened to stages of change subject to differing images and perceptions. Touraine's work (see chapter 2) leaves little doubt that the base of the movement and the leadership understood well the ultimate tie between authentic workers' rights and the demise of the party. On the other hand, while it is clear that those in the movement knew generally what they opposed, there remained the typical problem facing all resistance and revolutionary forces: a pragmatic program that would produce achievable results. That which emerged can be likened to a rational model of change in stages.

By late spring of 1981, Solidarity rhetoric and action focused on self-management. Though ambiguous, self-management appears in word and deed to have been imbued with two overriding meanings. First, it meant an end to the domination of the economy by the party and the *nomenklatura*. Toward this end, new management would introduce principles of economic rationalism to take the place of political influence. Secondly, Solidarity envisioned the institutionalization of self-management councils to be elected by workers (Touraine, 1981: 94-95). Touraine understates the case when he argues that Solidarity sought to break with earlier methods of industrial management. If placed in effect throughout Poland, such conceptions of self-management would have brought an end to central planning as well as to an economy driven by political command.

Independent trade unions and the right to strike were important tactical advances defined by many Poles as a means toward a greater measure of social justice. However, self-management, while a denunciation of a centrally planned economy, did not signify early on a commitment to a capitalist transformation. Indeed, the weakening of the center under state forms of socialism was already evident in what was then Yugoslavia, and found great support in the softer forms of Western Eurocommunism of the era. However, for the more visionary, such modifications were not sufficient unto themselves for the solution of the Polish crisis. As Touraine argued, the realization of free trade unions had as its precondition a larger debate and grand political struggle for the liberation of society. "It is as if the defence of free trade unions had to take place on ever widening ground" (Touraine, 1981: 86). This was evidenced in concrete terms in the debate within the National Coordinating Committee in the immediate months following the Gdansk strike. In the summer of 1981, the leadership of Solidarity was to move beyond narrowly defined workplace demands to a call for free elections. Toward this larger end, Solidarity would seek to enlarge its program, forcing the party-state to play its final card: that of martial law.

In the autumn of 1981, the militarization of Polish political structures began. Prior to this point, the party-state had been under civilian authority, with the military card played selectively to crush dissent and restore order. However, with Solidarity growing in size and influence, and with the rhetoric of self-management, democracy, and free elections sweeping the land, the authorities resorted to the last line of defense for a crumbling center of command. After Solidarity's Congress, Polish government came to resemble some of the more unstable regimes of Latin America. Rule by generals at the center was supplemented by the replacement or shoring up of local functionaries by Poles in uniform.

In concert with the militarization of the Polish state, Solidarity continued to articulate its demands. The demands were not really new: they included the routine call for access to the mass media, for free and democratic elections to local councils in the provinces, and for other parts of the program of workplace democracy and self-management. What was new became evident on December 12. To give teeth to its demands, Solidarity proposed a nationwide referendum on a noncommunist government, to be held if the regime refused its demands. On December 13, 1981, the regime imposed martial law. All strikes, demonstrations, and public meetings were banned, and a news blackout was enforced.

It is clear that Solidarity's leaders had not anticipated the severity of the crackdown and that the member base had not been prepared to tactically respond. When leaders issued a hasty call for a nationwide strike, only a few scattered work stoppages occurred. Walesa and other leaders were arrested. In retrospect, it is arguable that Solidarity leaders not only miscalculated the display of force on the part of a newly militarized regime, they also misread the will to strike on behalf of a clear and present break with communist rule. In coming to grips with this defeat for the resistance, it is crucial to remember that Solidarity had emerged in a dyadic context. On one level was the continuing systemic crisis that gripped Poland, a crisis clearly beyond the capacity of authorities to disguise, much less to manage. This continuing crisis gave encouragement and spurred the popularity of Solidarity as a resistance movement. However, it is one thing to be a member of a political community of discontent, bound together by opposition to a regime without popular legitimacy. It is quite another to act to bring down the existing order.

On the second, perhaps most important level, was the shadow of Soviet military power, now strongly tied to Polish martial force. It is impossible to overstate the symbolism and confusion introduced by Polish military rule. The prevailing fear was that the failure to restore order by force would bring rapid Soviet military intervention. On the other hand, the Polish military had its own credibility with many Poles. This consisted of more than the oft-cited romanticism Poles attribute to their military figures; it was also founded in the conviction that the military had stopped short of broad scale violence many times. Both of these views led to the same conclusion: it was better to have Polish martial law than Russian tanks. To these conditions must be added the ordinary and immense impediments in consciousness, will, and resources that stand as barriers to any social revolution. Taken together, these constraining factors had not served to limit the vision of broader change on the part of Solidarity's leadership, but they help account for the movement's faint and quickly negated response to the fateful events of December 1981. Although martial law was to be formally suspended in December of 1982, it was clear that any enlarged vision of Polish democracy would await other events.

Winston Churchill described his years out of power in an isolated Britain as the "wilderness years." The wilderness for *Solidarnosc* covered most of the decade of the 1980s, a time in which formal membership declined from ten to two million. Yet, it was during this period--when the Polish opposition labored in the shadow of a cross of iron--that the faithful learned the hard distinction between the abstracted idealism of liberty and the organizational toil required to sustain a movement of emancipation. During the Polish wilderness, joining and resisting were insufficient. Many Poles had known something of a

Hegelian freedom of the spirit emerging from the self-creation of resistance. Only a minority were active in the new learning, however. Those who participated discovered that Hegel was wrong. Human beings in bondage could not be free on any plane that endured without new structures that ended the objective relation between master and bondsman. It was fitting, therefore, that in this great process of collective discovery and self-education, movement democracy took the form of a vast organizational apparatus of forty thousand persons. Their salaries were paid from local dues so that there would be no doubt about the popular roots of authority--or in whose interest movement makers were seeking to fashion new roles, new rules, and new conceptions of social action. "Out of this self-generated world came the Network and its evolving plan for self-management, the Action Program, and the hundreds of local assertions through which self-organized communities endeavored to teach democratic conduct to each other and, collectively, to an authoritarian party apparatus" (Goodwyn, 1991: 348).

As is typically the case, the Polish story through the 1980s continued to be constructed by the world media, which focused on the occasional outbreak of high political drama. In the wake of martial law, Walesa and other leaders of Solidarity were arrested as a reminder of the Soviet-backed regime's recourse to the iron fist. When martial law was abandoned after a year, the Jaruzelski government demonstrated the politics of the velvet glove--announcing a series of reforms over the years while showing a moderate face to the dissidents. Walesa's credibility, and perhaps public safety, was secured in some significant measure by his selection for the Nobel Peace Prize in 1983.

The constant threat of Soviet intervention was well expressed in the grim joke: What country is surrounded on three sides by Russian tanks and the fourth by Russian cruisers? From a political standpoint, it is arguable that the most fateful condition for social transformation in Poland occurred in March of 1985, when Mikhail Gorbachev was selected as General Secretary of the Communist party in the former U.S.S.R. As the youngest member of the Politburo, his leadership role signaled a sharp reversal in the Stalinist policies of the old guard. With the introduction of glasnost and perestroika in 1987, it was clear that the U.S.S.R. would be preoccupied with trying to stave off both nationalism and economic crisis at an internal level. To the extent that Soviet systemic order, from the internal to the external levels, had rested in some significant measure on force or the threat of force, it was now clear that the old nemesis from the East would no longer dominate Poland. Still, the focus on appearances is not sufficient.

It is now possible to consider two seminal forces at play during the 1980s-- one dealing with macrostructural changes in political economy, and the other with the transformation of the Solidarity movement itself. These allow us to connect the Polish past and present. The first takes the form of what Kazimierz Poznanski terms the "restructuring of property rights" in Poland. While Poznanski's focus (1993) is perhaps legalistic, he does provide the basis for constructing the evolution of the Polish economy in the direction of privatization--a process that began well in advance of the fall of the Polish party-state.

During the period of the Gierek regime (1971-1980), the central state was strong in controlling the private sector, while arbitrary taxes and political decisions were a constant hazard. However, even during this decade, the central state (relative to earlier periods of regime history) was weak with regard to the exercise of command power from the top. Thus, even though public property was protected, low-level party units were playing a more crucial role in the economy. Following Poznanski, then, it can be argued that throughout the seventies, the Polish economy--though still driven by the ideology of real socialism and a protected private sector--was already undergoing a process of decentralization. If we add to this observation our findings from the previous chapter relating to the runaway Polish debt (and its false prosperity), it is plausible to argue that the seeds of broader systemic crisis and change were already planted well in advance of Solidarity.

During the Jaruzelski/Messner period (1981 to mid-1988), further change occurred. On the public sector side, there was evidence of further experimentation with "market" forces as the authorities attempted to move toward something resembling competition on prices and labor. However, state industries still held a monopolistic position in a highly regulated economy. On the private sector side, control was exercised by what Poznanski calls a "fractured bureaucratic structure." Private ownership rights were still poorly protected from a "parasitic state." In the brief Rakowski period (1988 to mid-1989), the public sector experiment with modified market forces continued, with the economic crisis expressed in a Polish-style stagflation. Although poor industrial and export performance were not new, the near-hyperinflation of this period sent shock waves through the economy. On the private side, the last gasp of the Polish party-state saw the emergence of weak market controls in the private sector, still small in size and also crippled by inflation. Private ownership remained without reliable legal protection, and the people came to view enterprises run by *nomenklatura* as corrupt. (The more recent problem of the newly capitalist *nomenklatura* will be taken up at a later point.)

SOLIDARITY CHANGES COURSE

Thus it was that the wilderness decade featured on the one side an economy that was neither fish or fowl, but one that was shifting, however slowly (and with mixed consequences), away from the Stalinist command model. As we shall see in due course, this structural ambivalence came to be defined in both the new circles of power and among the people themselves as the "cause" of the Polish economic crisis. Hence, it was to become an article of new ideological faith that the transformation should proceed at a radical pace toward privatization. The time was to be ripe for the coming of Western apostles of market extremism.

With the broad macroeconomic forces understood, we return to the transformation of Solidarity during the wilderness decade of the 1980s. Forces such as these must be articulated through intervening channels that affect both reality and consciousness. The movement that existed during the heady months of independence was to undergo its own transformation on the long road from Gdansk, and it is crucial to speak of these conditions with precision (Fields, 1991). As intimated above, the economic crisis and the fear of a liberation movement out of control spurred the party-state to enact martial law.

It is arguable that until that decisive moment in history, many Poles believed that it would be possible to move in the direction of a new democratized structure of self-management in stages. In September of 1981, a few months before martial law, the Solidarity Congress had advanced a program calling for workers' self-management at the factory level, local self-governing bodies, and a Chamber of Self-Management in the Polish Sejm. Quite clearly, it was not the negation of socialism but its decentralization that dominated political discourse at the level of Solidarity. On December 2, 1981, in a "rehearsal of martial law" (Fields, 1991: 108), the state resorted to strike breaking through force at Warsaw's Firefighter's Academy. Although "radicals" (such as Zbigniew Bujak) in Solidarity called for resistance in the form of mobilization and the creation of a provisional government, little happened other than talk. However, these are smaller issues. It was the overarching systemic crisis, expressed politically by Solidarity in calling for dramatic alterations in power relations, that ultimately brought martial law--with the corresponding threat to the disintegration of the union--and Solidarity's broad abandonment by many less committed supporters. How, then, would Solidarity survive?

The conventional view of Polish events during the 1980s has focused upon the conflict between the forces of the state and those of the resistance. This view is certainly defensible at the political and cultural levels, as labor unrest and confrontations in the context of Polish civil religion continued. However, what is routinely overlooked in the drama of power politics is the broader convergence of the interests and direction of both the established order and the "underground" Solidarity. Consider, for a moment, the macrostructural shift (see chapter 2) in the 1970s featuring large-scale development financed through debt to be repaid through exports. This reality meant that Poland was a participant in the world game of debt and dependency that included the national economies of Brazil, Mexico, Egypt, and a multitude of others (George, 1990: 1). Factor in the macroeconomic history briefly mentioned, which traces the ongoing transformation of the Polish economy from state command and toward market formations, however weak. Consider further the ongoing movement in Polish ruling circles toward Western conceptions of management (see chapter 2), the fascination with such having spread throughout the Soviet bloc. Recall also, that the rise of Gorbachev symbolized the clear discreditation of cumbersome central planning and a call for cost accounting, local management, and other reforms.

Thus, in the context of both world system and semiperipheral crises, the party-state in the U.S.S.R. was to begin to openly embrace a form of market socialism based upon the Western (especially American) capital-intensive, technologically driven, postindustrialist model. The conflict between the superpowers, routinely cast in terms of a struggle for military, political, or ideological hegemony, has the effect of obscuring the commitment on both sides to models of growth and modernization. This routinely unrecognized connection has a long history in the old U.S.S.R. In his work on the *State and Social Revolution*, Lenin declared that the vanguard need not reinvent the capitalist state but should put its organization in the service of the socialist revolution. The later Soviet planners and their junior partners throughout the East bloc had in parallel fashion long admired the organization and the efficiency of the large-scale Western corporation.

It is important to avoid mystification here. The typical response to these momentous events is to paint a glib picture of the emergence of a movement to establish Polish civil society. The truth, however, is both familiar and a bit more complex. Throughout the economies of Poland, Eastern Europe, and the U.S.S.R., living standards had continued their downward spiral from the mid-seventies. Gorbachev's quaint allusion (in his book, *Perestroika*) to a "braking mechanism" materializing in the 1970s, was for many in the Soviet orbit defined as a reverse gear driving Leninist style societies backward. No one knew this better than Walesa. In November of 1988, the Polish people saw a debate between the leader of Solidarity and a party hack and Politburo member, Alfred Miodowicz. Walesa called upon his own brand of realpolitik. "The West goes by car," he said, "and we're on a bike" (cited in Ash, 1991a: 52). The legitimation crisis had reached critical mass, but it continued to be fueled by the anxieties of survival.

Perhaps the great irony is that prior to martial law, Solidarity's threat was not merely to the regime but to the ongoing modernization and consolidation of the world market system. Its call for self-management and the realization of social justice in real terms not only would have preempted the domestic hegemony of the party-state, but seriously hampered the scale-back or elimination of heavy industry, as well as stalling the institutionalization of the "discipline" of unemployment (and underemployment) throughout the economy.

No claims are made here with regard to the "consciousness" (on either side of the relations of power) as to the nature of these higher forces. However, as noted in Fields (1991: 110), by 1983 "Solidarity underground publications such as Niepodleglosc (Independence) and Polityka Polska (Polish Politics) began to charge that Solidarity had been too socialist, too tied to faith in the power of the masses." Other writers (such as Andrzej Walicki and Piotr Wierzbicki) critiqued the movement for its anachronistic model and the ideological hegemony of the left. Jerzy Strzelecki made the transition from an advisor on self-management to a defender of private property, while Jerzy Milewski called for the transformation to a market economy. By April of 1987, the Solidarity underground leadership (the Provisional Coordinating Committee) "issued a document calling for extensive privatization of the economy (Fields, 1991: 111)." It is interesting to note that Solidarity survived the 1980s without a bloodbath and took the power of the state through peaceful negotiations. The conflict by that stage was not over whether there would be a transformation toward privatization, but over who would preside over the inevitable.

It was in this context of a curious structural commonality of interests that the tired regime attempted to restore legitimacy--but without the international or domestic credibility or credentials necessary for those who would administer change. For their part, Walesa and his advisors had avoided the road of an armed rising to travel one of patient willingness to negotiate. Throughout it all, the resistance benefited from constant international oversight, Soviet glasnost, the call for markets (whether market socialism or more radical privatization), and organizational ties that bonded the core of the opposition together.

Finally, during the decade of the 1980s, it was clear that the regime had been overtaken by the deeper forces of systemic crisis. As the Gorbachev policies made clear that massive external military force would not be used to maintain the old Polish order, the continuing pressures of economic decline and internal opposition pushed the regime and Solidarity toward a forum for conflict resolution. In late 1988, in the context of two waves of strikes by workers, Jaruzelski's regime followed a familiar road: that of signaling negotiations (Geremek, 1991). However, these talks were to produce what was heretofore an unthinkable end. The Round Table negotiations covered a two-month period from February 6 to April 4, 1989. The resulting agreements not only ended the oppression and resistance that marked rule by a militarized Polish state during the 1980s, they also brought to a close, for all practical purposes, four decades of Communist party power. [1]

Different mediators were used in the attempt to reach a negotiated political settlement to the Polish crisis, including the hierarchy of the Catholic church. A confidential meeting took place on August 31, 1988, in which Jaruzelski's interior minister, General Kiszczak, and Lech Walesa agreed on a range of questions, as well as on the overall purposes of negotiations and a range of procedural rules for the Round Table. Given both the history of martial law and the failure of political results from earlier negotiations as well as the highly symbolic liquidation of the Gdansk shipyard, many on the Solidarity side distrusted the sincerity of the regime.

---

[1]The following account was compiled by Krzysztof Polak from: 1) Dubinski, Krzysztof, Magdalenka - transakcja epoki. Notatki z poufnych spotkan Kiszczak - Walesa. Warszawa, BGW 1990; 2) Leski, Krzysztof, Cos czyli rzecz o okraglym stole. Warszawa Wydawnictwo Grup Oporu "Solidarnosci" 1989; 3) Okragly Stol oprac. J. Barszczewski, J. Grochalska. Warszawa PAP 1989, Zeszyty Dokumentacyjne PAP, Red. Zagraniczna Seria Monograf. 7-8, 9-10; 4) Smolenski, Pawel: Szermierze Okraglego Stolu: zwatpienie i nadzieje. Wydawnictwo "Most" 1989; 5) Porozumienia Okraglego Stolu. Warszawa, 6.02 - 5. 04, 1989. Olsztyn NZSS "Solidarnosc" Rejon Warminsko - Mazurski; 6) Porozumienia Okraglego Stolu: dyskusja plenarna, dokumenty, notatki. Warszawa, Rada Krajowa PRON 1989.

A number of such preliminary meetings took place before the deliberations of the Round Table began. Some of the encounters took place in Magdalenka, a village near Warsaw, where a small recreation center of the Polish Home Secretary was located. Hence, the secret talks were termed the "Magdalenkas" by some. A significant turn of events took place after the X plenary session of the Communist party, as important staff changes saw the rise of reformers hoping to ensure some place for the party in the changing currents that were sweeping Poland and the U.S.S.R. In the chaos of increasing strikes and the real threat of a general work stoppage, increasing inflation, and market shortages, the fear of an immanent social explosion was more than idle speculation. Power would be shared or lost completely.

Threatened by the resignations of realists such as Jaruzelski, Kiszczak, Rakowski, and Siwicki, who understood that the status quo could not be maintained, most members of the Central Committee agreed to the Round Table talks. The official deliberations began on February 6, 1989, in the Palace of Ministers in Warsaw. General Kiszczak opened the plenary meeting by formally proposing a model and overall objectives for the negotiations. Walesa accepted for the Solidarity side, and the participants broke up into working groups. Negotiations were conducted on such issues as trade unions, pluralism, political reforms, economic change, and social policy. The opening and concluding plenary sessions were restricted to 57 participants, but some 433 persons--including additional experts and advisors--participated in the working groups.

Many of the issues to be negotiated at the Round Table were not new. Representatives addressed the rising prices of food (chronically associated with a dramatic decline in the standard of living) and the rate of indexation of payments, the rules of nonconfrontational elections, the restoration and structure of the institutions of the Senate and presidency, and the retraction of dismissals and other forms of repression directed toward strikers. While Warsaw was the venue for the official talks, a parallel and underground round table continued in the confidential meetings at Magdalenka. It was here that representatives of the church played an important and facilitating role.

As noted by B. Geremek, the agents of a fading regime were now facing representatives from Solidarity's major streams: a triple alliance of workers, peasants, and intellectuals. Although the church's official position was that of mediation, it was clear to all that these talks symbolically took place in the shadow of the cross. And although there is no evidence of direct orchestration, the demonstration of popular protest and response throughout the talks served to remind the generals of the limitations of martial force. Solidarity the union and Solidarity the movement had progressed in an almost imperceptible fashion: from reaction and rebellion to a new quasi-institutional standing of initiative and public pressure. For there was now something new in Polish history: a populace demanding more than the right to be heard, more than the right to answer back. The demand to legalize Solidarity was also a demand for elections. However immature and however faint, a new discourse requiring new channels for the exercise of political power was abroad in the land.

On the fifth of April, an agreement was reached that called for the recognition of Solidarity and its press along with a compromise on the question of free elections. In the new Sejm, 65 percent of members would be drawn from a coalition of the signatories to PRON (Patriotyczny Ruch Ocalenia Narodowego), the Patriotic Movement of National Salvation, comprised of the Communist party and its allies. The remaining 35 percent were open to the opposition. The date of the election was fixed for the first week of June, as the regime believed that the opposition would not be able to organize so quickly. However, this proved to be an enormous miscalculation. The opposition won 99 of 100 seats in the Senate and 160 of the 161 open positions in the Sejm.

On the evening of the sixth of June, the Communist party of Poland acknowledged electoral defeat and vowed to accept the political consequences. Despite official ideology denouncing bourgeois elections, it can be argued that longtime party leaders and members were sobered--if not devastated--by the massive repudiation of their leadership in a "workers' state." The long standing cliche that the opposition was composed of deviants and reactionaries was rendered absurd, unless virtually all of Poland so qualified. The party, however, did not so meekly keep its pledge. In what Lawrence Goodwyn (1991: 351) called perestroika Polish style, Jaruzelski played musical political chairs. He moved himself from party first secretary to president, C. Kiszczak from interior minister to prime minister, and M. Rakowski to first secretary. However, then came the quiet insurrection in the Sejm. Defections by members of the Peasants and Democratic parties gave Solidarity the votes to reject Kiszczak as prime minister. The genie was out of the bottle. Whatever the difficulties ahead in defining and building the institutions of civil society, the Polish opposition seized the moment. In the second week of August, one of the early core of intellectuals at Gdansk rose from movement leader to institutional prominence. With the support of Walesa and the new converts to change, Tadeusz Mazowiecki was elected the new prime minister of Poland.

So it was that in the spring of 1989, the legal existence of an opposition movement, now a party clearly destined to take the power of the state, was recognized in what had been a Soviet satellite. The Round Table had succeeded where so many efforts had failed before. It replaced accusation and cynicism with the direct bargaining that leads to institutional power sharing. However, given the momentous events shaking the whole U.S.S.R. and all of Eastern Europe, the Round Table must be seen as the first of a series of funeral services for an old order already doomed to death by the irresolvable contradictions of systemic crisis.

In this fateful year the Round Table and subsequent Polish elections combined to constitute a symbolic and precipitating factor in wider and almost immediate events. In Hungary, border fences blocking access to the West soon fell and East Germans used that nation as a corridor to reach the West. East Germany, which had also traveled the road of development through massive debt, faced its own rendezvous with change. On October 18, Erich Honecker was forced to resign in the face of nationwide protest, on November 4 the border with Czechoslovakia was opened to refugees, and on November 9 the decision to open the border to the West signaled the end of the Berlin Wall--a barrier that had stood since 1961. In Czechoslovakia, tens of thousands took to the streets of Prague on November 17, and the party leadership resigned on November 24. On December 10, a new cabinet took power--a cabinet with a noncommunist majority. On December 29, Vaclav Havel, a playwright whose words and deeds had given heart so often to campaigners for human rights, was elected president. And so it was throughout Eastern Europe, with the political denouement coming on Christmas day, 1991, when Mikhail Gorbachev, whose vision exceeded the reach of an imploding order, resigned. The hammer and sickle was lowered in a second world--where the center did not hold.

BEYOND POLITICS: THE DILEMMA OF THE NEW POLISH STATE

It has been said that success has many fathers, while failure is an orphan. In the summer of 1989, the dizzying success of Polish union, founded on nationalism and resistance against common forces as well as a strange alliance based on social justice and market ideology, knew no shortage of ancestors. But there is a wide abyss between the organization of a movement and the formation of state governance, between an ideology of resistance and a program of action, between the glittering and undefined values of democracy and privatization and the realities of political economy. It would take more than a consciousness of domination, more than faith and nation, more than a successful struggle against all odds to hold Solidarity together. Poles from all walks of life had known for centuries the identity of those who opposed them; thus the emergence of an almost endless series of campaigns to save the nation, a struggle symbolically reflected in the anthem "Poland Is Not Yet Lost." It would prove a far more daunting task to forge a new and proactive consensus. Yet, as we shall see, to conceptualize the barriers to a new Polish state and civil society as those of consensus building is both shallow and a form of evasion.

There was admittedly, almost from the beginning of the new order, a failure of political consensus. Western observers saw in Poland (as in much of the former East bloc) a disarray reflected in a plethora of parties and recourse to shifting parliamentary alliances in order to carry an agenda that seemed to change by the moment. They saw a fracturing of the Solidarity alliance, with Walesa and his more trusted Gdansk advisors locked in the conflicts of realpolitik with Mazowiecki and the "Warsaw intellectuals" such as Michnik and Geremek. The break began early, when in the late summer of 1989, Mazowiecki appeared reluctant to consult Walesa on appointments and policy. Walesa complained that Western journalists had contemptuously reduced him to a limited symbol, an electrician with delusional ambitions (Ash, 1991a: 53). Such perceptions notwithstanding, Walesa enjoyed ideological stature in conservative Western circles--confirmed by journeys to Ronald Reagan's America and Margaret Thatcher's Britain, in addition to having received the aforementioned Nobel Peace Prize. He thus remained the most visible symbol of Poland's national wish to do more than merely survive tyranny. He trounced both Mazowiecki and the mysterious Stan Tyminski, who brought the curious credentials of an erstwhile self-made millionaire (a poorer version of the United States' Ross Perot) to the 1990 campaign for the presidency. However, the president of the Republic of Poland was to preside over parliamentary chaos featuring a succession of prime ministers and other notables committed to one or another version of fast-track privatization. Further, behind the new public crisis in political authority loomed the rapidly escalating structural crisis of inequality.

In vital ways, the mass appeal of the Solidarity movement in the 1980s transected occupational and status lines in Poland. It is arguable that the very universality of the appeal, while effective at a movement level, could only break apart with the fracturing of interests at the institutional phase. For many Poles--peasants, miners, and especially the industrial workers at the core of Solidarity--the movement was legitimated by its egalitarian ideals. After the seizure of state power, the formerly allied forces of resistance found themselves on the horns of a dilemma. What can be called the fast track to a market system assumed that economic development would follow laissez-faire Polish capital accumulation. Hence the price to be paid for greater development would be greater inequality (supposedly only for the near term). Both the many supporters and the few critics of privatization tended to share the strongly entrenched view in Poland that capitalism must be built with a human face and that the problems of unemployment, underemployment, and poverty were only to be a stage in the transition. And herein lies the crux of the great and contemporary divide that marks modern Poland. In large, but certainly not exclusive measure, the Polish dilemma is rooted in the conflict between growth and distribution; between models of economic and human development; between the ideals of prosperity for the upwardly mobile and those of social justice at a national level. To the extent that this dilemma is ignored or institutionalized, a massive upheaval awaits.

Ironically enough, it was Walesa himself who came to personify this new dichotomy in Polish society. On the more visible side of political life, he toured the United States, Great Britain, and the wealthier nations of Europe seeking investment capital and acquiring some identity as a "Polish Thatcherite," due to his professions of admiration for the "iron lady" (Ash, 1991b). On the more intimate, domestic side, his proposals for radical privatization at home offered some vision (however rhetorical) of ownership for every Pole, while offering the assurances of justice, faith, and nationalism that had worked so well during the 1980s. It would be simplistic to dismiss this behavior as that of the political chameleon, doing whatever is necessary to curry favor and win the next election. Walesa is best understood as the personal and symbolic embodiment of the Polish dilemma.

The drama of taking and using the power of the state often mystifies forces that are beyond the reach of politics. The tendency to reduce the stresses and strains of institutionally founded conflict to the level of private lives--and the personalities of luminaries--is the essence of soap opera journalism and insider-based accounts of popular history. The political theater of resistance to Soviet rule in Poland galvanized media, popular, and many academic perceptions in the West. It was as if Poland and its people existed not in their own right but as players in some universal morality play destined to prove the ultimate triumph of Western good over Soviet evil. But just as the focus on heroism and mythmaking missed the higher story of legitimation and systemic crisis during the movement phase of Solidarity, so has this poverty of explanation plagued comprehension of the transformation itself. Thus it is that reductive accounts of personal power struggles and individual deficiencies have blended too well with elitist stereotypes about Poland and social change.

It is simply too convenient to attribute the hard travail of the Polish transformation to petty squabbles between intellectuals and workers, to jealousies afflicting Walesa and his rivals for insider power, or to differences in the legislative agendas of one alliance of parties or another. It is also somewhat shallow to attribute the new legitimation crisis to inexperience or to assumed deficiencies in Polish institutional history. Of course there are to be found, in Polish governing circles, the usual petty differences that mushroom into high-profile squabbles and often bitter personal attacks. Correspondingly, it is true enough that the absence of civil society and market experience (whatever the critical problematics revealed by the deconstruction of these terms) continue to plague the Polish transformation. However, to understand both the peril and promise of the transformation requires us to take higher theoretical ground.

The macrostuctural barriers to authentic legitimacy and systemic transformation fall into two essential categories: those that are general and those that are specific to the Polish situation. During the first years, mid-1989 to September, 1993, of new rule (Mazowiecki/Bielecki and then Walesa/Suchocka), the twin pillars of economic transformation emerged in the form of rapid privatization and open trade. These articles of faith were embraced by virtually every faction, with even the communists voting in favor of the privatization of large state-owned enterprises (to become effective in 1994.) However, the Polish introduction to the market was for many a rude awakening. The ideology of free trade proved more tranquilizing than substantive for Polish exporters. As reported in the *New York Times* on September 23, 1993 (A-22), during the early nineties the West hauled out the usual barriers required to protect powerful national economies and put the squeeze on Polish exports, especially agricultural products. Steel manufacturers and textile mills were also hit hard by the Western refusal to buy.

A second external dimension of the ongoing Polish crisis is revealed in the role played by the Bretton Woods organizations - specifically, the International Monetary Fund (IMF) and the World Bank. The IMF in the early nineties established performance standards designed to accelerate the rate of Polish privatization in return for the release of desperately needed new money. This step was linked to developmental funding from the World Bank and other multilateral organizations as well as Western governments (*The Economist*,

March 27, 1993: 55-56). (One major privatization trade-off was to be massive unemployment.)

If huge transnational actors in the world market system drove the Polish transformation on an external plane, more intimate players brought the gospel of free enterprise and big-bang privatization to Poland. "Shock therapists" such as Harvard's Jeffrey Sachs came first to Poland (and later to the U.S.S.R.) to recommend "reforms." Shock therapy, or the radical conversion to capitalism, began in January of 1990. The fact that the program was driven more by faith and ideology than by rational assessment was evident from the start. "Marketization" ignored the dilemma faced by Polish banks and suppliers with their insufficient credit to advance to the fledgling private sector; it operated on the faith position that external investment flows would fund privatization--when those who controlled those flows insisted that a large measure of privatization come first; it assumed that the conversion from a centralized, bureaucratized command economy was a matter of simple reeducation and political will; it assumed that it was necessary to destroy the Polish economy in order to save it. The statistics disguise massive cruelty.

In November of 1989, a series of forecasts emerged from Warsaw. Output was predicted to fall by 5 percent in six months, setting the stage for recovery and growth. The reality was that industrial production fell by 25 percent in the first quarter of 1990 alone, continuing to shrink into mid-1993, although at a more modest rate. The zloty was set at 9,500 to the U.S. dollar, and inflation was predicted to slow to Western levels in a year or two. By mid-1993, inflation had reached an annual level of 40 percent and the zloty floated to a level of 16,290 to the dollar (Hanks and Walters, 1993: 52). By midyear of 1994, the rate was over 22,000 zlotys to 1 U.S. dollar (*International Herald Tribune*, June 30, 1994: 1).

The advance of privatization is difficult to assess, especially in issues relating to employment and gross domestic product (GDP), because of changing definitions of the "new" and "old" private sector. However, the total number of private firms registered to do business in Poland rose from 857,430 in 1989 to some 1.7 million in early 1993. It is crucial to point out that over 90 percent (1.6 million) of these firms are run by private individuals using their own savings and are thus not legally defined as companies. The number of state firms in the public sector declined from 7,337 in 1989 to 6,838 in the first quarter of 1993. About one in four state firms by this point had started along one of a number of tracks toward privatization, although one-fourth of this number had been transformed into joint-stock firms owned by the State Treasury (Vinton, 1993: 58).

Although state involvement continues to be naively criticized, it is difficult to build capitalism without capital, and few external investors are interested unless "value" is to be had. By mid-1993, the real level of total foreign investment committed to Poland over four years averaged some $1 billion per annum (Vinton, 1993: 59-60). By way of comparison, U.S. direct investment abroad in 1993 exceeded $548 billion (World Almanac, 1995: 125.) A single investment by Fiat in Poland, with its purchase of the FSM auto plant in

Tychy, resulted in a pledge to invest $1.8 to $2 billion over an eight-year period. This, combined with the purchase of Huta Warszawa (now the Lucchini steel mill), made Italy the leader in pledged investment--with the United States in second position and Germany not in the running at all (Vinton, 1993: 61-62). Whether such pledges will be realized or whether investment increases in the future depend on the volatility of the Polish crisis. The plague of external debt has also continued to hang heavy despite some relief evidenced in early 1994. Between 1970 and 1980, long-term public debt in Poland grew from only $24 million U.S.D. to $6.6 billion. By 1991, this form of debt had increased by almost 600 percent to $44.1 billion. Adding in the use of IMF credit and short-term debt instruments, total external debt for Poland in 1991 reached $52.5 billion with total arrears (principal and interest not paid) reaching $11.3 billion (World Bank, 1991: 245; 1993: 279). As reported by the Associated Press on March 12, 1994, this sum had reached almost $12 billion when the debt was restructured. Commercial banks agreed to reduce the total amount in arrears by 42-45 percent. This provided some necessary breathing room, but the Polish debt crisis remained far from over.

At the level of the general Polish population, economic decline translated into an unemployment rate of one worker in six by the end of 1993, introducing the question of the degree of pauperization and inequality. In November of 1993, the European Community (EC) reported that some small upward change in GDP (from its highly depressed level) was feasible, that there were indications of an "improved work ethic," and that a value-added tax on consumption had been successfully introduced. At the political level, the 1993 election reduced the twenty-nine parties to a total of six. The EC (now European Union) "estimated" that 20 percent of Poles were doing well, 20 percent were doing poorly, and the rest were in limbo as to the benefits of the market economy (Europe, 1993). Although hard data is difficult to obtain, as of mid-1993 it was possible to draw some tentative conclusions concerning the short-term effects of "shock therapy" in Poland on inequality and poverty.

Bozena Leven (1993: 237-43), drawing on measures of income distribution (percentage share of household income by quintiles for nonagricultural workers, farmers, and retirees), total household savings deposits, average percentage of monthly income spent on foodstuffs, and quarterly unemployment rates--concludes that the benefits of marketization have yet to be felt by most Poles. The "income distribution disparities" appeared to have worsened for nonagricultural workers (who constitute 66 percent of the total labor force), with incrementally small improvements in the distribution among farmers and retirees. However, the question of distribution overlooks the larger reality of the pauperization of society. The ideologized view of communism in the West previously held that members of Soviet style societies could only expect to experience an equality of national scarcity. It is ironic that this observation perhaps better fits the response to shock therapy for the Polish economy and necessarily, for Polish society. It is not simply that some Poles are getting more and some less. It is also that the economic pie became much smaller, giving a harsher edge to the competitive struggle for existence. Especially hard hit was the manufacturing sector. With an index of 100 for the year 1980, earnings per employee dropped from 114 in 1989 to 78 in 1990 to 76 in 1991 (World Bank, 1994: 175).

A qualitative and somewhat ethnographic view of the early consequences of shock therapy is offered by Paul Zarembka who described the new policies as a "disaster for ordinary people" (1993: 21). Some observers argued that Poland had achieved capitalism, but an eighteenth- or nineteenth-century model. Another insider complained that Poland had gone from a stupid government to one that is more stupid. Strong disaffection was expressed in many quarters with regard to Solidarity and its leaders. In the summer of 1992, six major unions (not including Solidarity), were backing demands similar to those from the Polish August of 1980 (see chapter 3 in this volume). "Their proposals included, among others: (1) set economic policy in the national interest, (2) eliminate unemployment, (3) end privatization, (4) stop selling factories to foreign capital, and (5) preserve the domestic market for domestically produced goods" (Zarembka, 1993: 25). Other criticisms concerned the shifting role of the church--from a bastion of Polish nationalism and some support for Solidarity to an advocate for religious instruction in the schools and the banning of abortion. (The antiabortion issue becomes crucial given the prospective pressure of larger families on declining resources.) Whatever one says about the pessimism of these observations, the rolling thunder of unemployment touching one worker in five yields support to a more ominous view.

Of course, there are other images. John Darnton's (1993) observations as London bureau chief of the *New York Times* juxtapose the new symbols of change. On the one side is the new Okecie airport at Warsaw, the proliferation of hotels and McDonalds, the popularity of U.S. movies and English language instruction (replacing Russian), the ubiquitous billboards, the booming Polish film industry, and Western-style discotheques. On the other side one finds a darker imagery. In addition to massive unemployment, Poland is enduring the emergence of skinheads; streets filled with hordes of poor Romanians, Russians, Moldavians, Ukranians and others; plentiful apartments market priced at from $15,000 to $80,000 (with an average monthly wage of under $200); and the decline of the textile industry in Lodz (resulting in the close of 132 of 285 factories and the layoffs of 40,000 persons between 1990 and the end of 1993.).

While descriptive accounts are useful, it is necessary to connect the personal and the public, the biographical and the historical, the symbolic and the real. The icons of Western modernization, ranging from airports to hotels, from shops to cultural imports, are reminiscent of similar development in Bangkok, Manila, Sao Paulo, Bogota and many urban centers throughout the developing world. In the Warsaw Holiday Inn, managed by the Bass European group headed by the multibillionaire Bass brothers of Fort Worth, Texas, a room can be had--for about a month's wages for the average Pole. But the luxury hotels, complete with CNN and MTV broadcasts, are not for the vast majority of Poles. They are for business travel and foreign tourists. On the other side of the hardening new relations in Poland, the skinheads from Nowa Huta are from the same marginalized working class as their alienated and troubled counterparts in the West.

The question of the reproduction of a class system is compounded by factors specific to the Polish situation. Among the more intriguing of these is the current role of some members of the old Communist party *nomenklatura* who have proven remarkably adroit in adapting to the new world of private markets. The new and ardent capitalists exploited their credentials, capital, networks, and general knowledge of bureaucracies to cash in on the shift in power. This transition may not have been a difficult one. From the 1970s, the *nomenklatura* had access to the special stores, dachas, and Western goods formerly available only to top officials (Rosenberg, 1993). For these, the Marxist dictum of "from each according to his ability, to each according to his need" had become "from each according to his party connections, to each according to what he could grab." The point is that corruption--as well as certain of the vestiges of capitalism (including heavy reliance on material incentives)--came to Poland before the Round Table talks.

Although a popular scapegoat for the present crisis in Poland, the success of the former communists cannot be understood in isolation. Paradoxically, the shock therapy program mentioned above (named in 1990 for finance minister Leszek Balcerowicz) worked to the benefit of the "reformed" *nomenklatura*. In addition to the elimination of price controls and subsidies came a fire sale on state-owned assets. "Many government and industry officials dramatically undervalued their companies and then sold them to their friends and relatives, or bought the companies themselves" (Rosenberg, 1993: 50). None of this was illegal. The breakneck speed of privatization meant that only those Poles with connections, capital, import-export expertise, and some experience in the management of complex organizations would be in a position to prosper from the move to markets. As shares of stock are offered in the wake of continued privatization, a pattern is emerging that may only intensify. Hard-pressed workers are selling their shares to managers. The simple irony is that former party hacks are sometimes the only Poles to get ahead. Given a wider view, it may not matter whether the *nomenklatura* or other more "honest" Poles are doing the buying. More serious and complex is the realization that this process of intensifying class formations was only further dividing Poland into a society separate and unequal.

As inviting as it may be, however, to make old communists into current villains, the current Polish crisis cannot be resolved by scapegoating and conspiracy theory. Poland has found itself in the throes of a cowboy style of capitalism that would be considered bizarre even in the laissez faire United States, much less the more sedate market economies of the nations of the European Union, with their strong social democratic institutions. Pauperization aside, even the contribution of private capital to the new Polish economy has had unanticipated consequences for Polish workers, so many of whom supported Solidarity in the heady time of the Polish August. Privatization may be said to have adversely affected the will to strike, even when conditions are hard. It is paradoxical that in the old Poland, strikes brought the fear of political and (on occasion) martial retaliation, but because of full employment policies, strikes did not result in massive loss of jobs. Given the "market discipline" of the New Poland, plants may be sold, privatized, or closed, and workers may find themselves joining the massive ranks of the unemployed. A primal economic fear may thus be said to have replaced the fear of political tyranny as paralyzing the will to strike at least in the near term. It is within this context that Solidarity, the proud union and movement of resistance, has experienced division and decline.

The new legitimation crisis in Poland is evidenced in the regression of Solidarity, both in organizational and ideological terms. Workers, fearful of losing what little they have, demonstrate less and less of the will to strike unless their enterprise appears on the brink of insolvency. After the 1991 elections, the twenty-six deputies (of the Sejm) along with the ten senators who together comprised the Solidarity Parliamentary Caucus reported to the National Commission at the top.

The leadership at both levels, having come to preside over an increasingly regionalized and disparate membership, conducted union business at the level of the state. Solidarity's leaders and former activists, now holding the power of the state, joined the tide of privatization--lending their support, for example, to the Pact on State Enterprises (Kimbell, 1993). By the summer of 1993, the handwriting was on the wall. Walesa had formed a Non-Party Bloc to cooperate more fully with the government headed by Prime Minister Hanna Suchocka in the drive toward "marketization." The Solidarity Congress, representing the rank and file, condemned the new economic reforms and censored those of the Solidarity Parliamentary Caucus who had voted to support them. Walesa declared that he did not want to belong to the "present Solidarity." One of the icons of Polish history had ridden a wave of organized resistance to state tyranny to reach the pinnacle of power. Once installed, he and others of the new officialdom discovered that the road from Gdansk did not end at the zenith but continued on toward the nadir of vanquished hopes and broken dreams. The crisis of the Polish state was again to be addressed by a changing of the guard.

Three months after Walesa formed the bloc rebuffed by the Solidarity Congress, the Polish electorate went to the polls for the third time since the Round Table. When the votes were counted on September 20, 1993, the urban-based Democratic Left Alliance (SLD) and the Polish Peasant Party emerged--prepared to control two-thirds of the seats in the Sejm. (The Democratic Left Alliance, composed of the Social Democracy of the Republic of Poland and the former official OPZZ trade union federation, is known as the postcommunist alliance.) The SLD, led by former officials of the former Polish party-state, together with an old rural party with communist roots, had taken some 36 percent of the popular vote. The Democratic Union of Prime Minister Hanna Suchocka, headed by old Solidarity activists, had won only 10.5 percent of the vote with only three others among the myriad of parties gaining the required 5 percent threshold for seats in parliament. One of these was the Non-Party Bloc of Lech Walesa, which stumbled from the ballot boxes with 5.4 percent of the vote. Of the emerging left coalition, 61 of 171 seats came to be controlled by the OPZZ which "succeeded the almost-defunct Solidarity as Poland's largest trade-union organization" (*Economist*, 1994: 56).

Perhaps most striking of the results of the 1993 election was the rejection of the Fatherland Catholic Election Coalition favored by the church. Although winning 6.4 percent of the vote, it failed to reach the 8 percent level required of an amalgam party. In an ironic twist, the Left Alliance had gained support from educated young people, including many women, who were drawn to its pledge to overturn earlier antiabortion legislation promoted by the church (Perlez, 1993a). The Solidarity government in its various forms and alliances had secured the support of the church, not only by pushing through a strict abortion law but also by a statute asserting Christian values and provisions allowing Catholic instruction in the public schools, though on a voluntary basis (*Economist*, 1994: 56). (These measures, along with the provisions of a concordat with the Vatican passed by the Suchocka government on the eve of her resignation - asserting church authority in matters of marriage and divorce and largely exempting the church from taxation - were being politically challenged in 1994.) Hence it was that the Polish legitimation crisis, driven by a looming systemic crisis yet to be understood, had come full circle. In the larger scheme of Polish things, Solidarity and the church, the twin pillars of opposition to the old hegemony, had fallen far from political grace.

On the eighthteenth of October 1993, Waldemar Pawlak of the Polish Peasant Party (PSL) became Prime Minister of Poland. Ironically, Pawlak had won one of the 76 parliamentary seats reserved for the United Peasant Party under the Round Table agreement of 1989. This party was the forerunner of the Polish Peasant Party, and Pawlak had supported its separation from communist allies and allied the organization with Solidarity in bringing Prime Minister Tadeusz Mazowiecki to power. In 1993, the PSL capitalized on several forces, to become the linchpin of the left coalition. First, it benefited from the support founded in the Polish peasantry, threatened with extinction by new forms of capital-intensive agriculture. The PSL won nearly 50 percent of the rural vote, taking much of the support that had gone to Solidarity-allied rural parties in 1991. Second, the PSL had a much softer image than the SLD, still considered a *nomenklatura* party. And third, the rural members of the PSL were traditionally closer to the church teachings than the more urbanized and educated constituency of the SLD.

Despite the political significance of the role of the PSL as power broker between postcommunist and post-Solidarity forces, the Democratic Left Alliance took control of the nation's economic policies in the fall of 1993. Led by Aleksander Kwasniewski, the Alliance declared its commitment to the ongoing transformation toward a market economy and the rules of democratic order. Most significantly, however, the new ideology emerged as one of social democracy--far closer in tone and rhetoric to the states of the European Union than to the chaos of unfettered privatization (Vinton, 1993). In a twist on the Prague Spring of 1968, Kwasniewski as an eclectic "man of the left" called repeatedly for a market economy "with a human face" (Perlez, 1993b: A6). If there was a sunny side to the Polish economic slide, it was that the economy had grown by some 4.5 percent in 1993 (*Christian Science Monitor,* February 16, 1994).   However, as the elections had made clear, from the perspective of many of the Polish people, this improvement had been built on the bottom of massive decline.

The two governing parties in 1994 formed an uneasy coalition, reflecting the structural contradictions in Polish economy and society. The PSL was committed to addressing the needs of Polish farmers, with perhaps a third in increasingly desperate circumstances. While a World Bank model (endorsed by Poland's new business elite) called blithely for a movement from agriculture to industry and services, this hope ignored the official unemployment rate of 16 percent. Put bluntly, there were no such jobs to absorb the small family farmers. On a familiar theme, the new government continued to face pressure from the International Monetary Fund to keep the state deficit at 4.1 percent of gross domestic product. Thus, the imperative to contain the threat of hyperinflation through the familiar austerity measures continued to contradict the political pledges to ease the pain of economic reform.

After months of debate, Prime Minister Pawlak signed the legislation authorizing the Polish privatization plan in October of 1994 (*Christian Science Monitor*, October 24, 1994: 4). Ultimately, the plan called for the staged privatization of 1,000 industrial firms. Initially, some 444 enterprises were to be distributed among some twelve to fifteen National Investment Funds. Funds were to be managed by consortia of foreign and Polish firms responsible for converting the enterprises to private status through arranging for capital and technology infusion as well as marketing and management skills. The state retained 25 percent of the stock of the enterprises, employees received 15 percent and foreign companies and Polish partners held the 60 percent remainder. However, the role of foreign firms in the consortia of fund managers reveals again the dilemma of dependence on foreign capital. These firms are service in nature and do not risk capital in Poland.

Perhaps the most optimistic of indicators in mid-decade were two developments. One was an increasingly aggressive posture on the part of Poland (as well as Hungary, Slovakia, and the Czech Republic) that the European Union expand eastward--and that concrete membership negotiations begin in the near future. The second was the decision to build toll highways at a cost of $8 billion over fifteen years. The infrastructure program was expected to create some 150,000 jobs. Not only was this move necessary given the condition of roadways, it was symbolic in that essential public works projects must be a vital component of the developmental hopes of Poland.

However laudable the ideals of social justice--including the calls for higher taxes for the rich, reducing tax incentives for business, higher pensions, more money for health and education, and increases in state subsidies for enterprises-- these are internal tactics that continue to wax and wane in the whirlwind of Polish politics. It is precisely these measures, which are arguably so crucial for the survival of ordinary Poles, that are defined by Darwinian marketeers as counterproductive. Only a critical examination of external relations, which are driven by higher systemic forces, will enable us to better contextualize and understand the Polish paradox of change. And it is to this task that we now turn.

Chapter 4

Development and Misdevelopment: Poland and the New World Order

To this point, the Polish situation has been contextualized in a relational view of history--with specific emphasis on the long struggle for national existence against rival European powers, institutional incorporation during the Soviet era into the COMECON alliance, and the creeping absorption of Poland and the East bloc into the world market system. This consideration of the larger questions of milieu is crucial for understanding the drama of Polish internal affairs, including decades of labor, peasant, and intellectual unrest and resistance. The rising tide of Polish discontent culminated in the founding of Solidarity as a union, its rapid transformation into a broader movement, and its survival in the wilderness years of the decade. This remarkable movement reached its zenith at the Round Table events in 1989 and its nadir in the September elections of 1993. The defeat of the Suchocka government and the failure of Walesa's Non-Party Bloc in the context of mounting economic, political, and social crisis only gave expression to the obvious. Solidarity could not be simultaneously a force for social justice and the engine of radical marketization.

There is one part of the contemporary saga yet to be explored. The coming of capitalism to Poland has redefined its relations with Western institutions and organizations. The fast track to a market economy, political democracy, and the institutions of civil society is not merely an internal affair under the direction of the new Polish authorities. The transformation of Poland has been aided and abetted by intergovernmental organizations, by national governments, by private investors and international banks, and by a legion of Western consultants advising on the formation of new Polish institutions. The Western "program" for Poland is one of development--and the shape and direction of that program follows a model commonly known as modernization.

THE DIALECTICS OF MODERNIZATION

In 1990, Alvin So argued that modernization theory in Western thought can be contextualized historically in three crucial events: the emergence of the United States as a superpower, the spread of a world movement toward communism, and the decolonization of former European empires, with the resultant emergence of many newly independent political states. "In such historical context, it was natural that American political elites encouraged their social scientists to study the Third World nation-states, to promote economic development and political stability in the Third World, so as to avoid losing the new states to the Soviet communist bloc" (So, 1990: 17). This chapter will be guided by the addition of a fourth event of global proportions: the decline and fall of the Soviet Union and the collapse of communist power in the states of Eastern Europe. This event did not contribute to the rise of modernization theory as much as to its relegitimation--with a vengeance.

Modernization thought in the social sciences must first be reviewed before we consider the ways in which this design is being employed from the outside and inside as a means of driving the transformation of Poland. Although the Polish situation is distinctive in many ways from conditions facing nations of the southern hemisphere, the issues of development are sometimes held in common. Modernization thought in the social sciences can be seen both as ideology (a legitimation system for Western-style institutional and cultural transformation) and as an explanatory system seeking to identify and assess the forces and processes that change traditional societies along social, cultural, political, and, above all, economic dimensions.

Social modernization focuses on such transitions as urbanization, the decline of traditional authority, and broadly conceived educational changes that result in differentiation--hence the fragmentation of institutions along the lines of specialization and heterogeneity. Thus conceived, social institutions and organizations are assumed to evolve toward a high level of interdependence, and social relations should become progressively *gesellschaft* in nature. Cultural modernization is ordinarily cast in the West as a movement from the sacred to the secular and the replacement of family, clan, tribal, or communal forms of identity with allegiance to a higher-order nation. (Given centuries of nationhood, this traditional view of third world societies and culture does not address the Polish situation directly. However, the issue of cultural transformation as a form of development can and will be reconfigured.) Political forms of modernization encompass the development of institutions of civil society--especially those of representative and participatory democracy-- intended to guarantee voting rights, parties, and parliaments. Administration as an ideal type is assumed to be bureaucratized and free of nepotism, and countervailing power is to be assured by such devices as the stratification and checks provided by a variety of governmental units (ranging from local to center) and organized interest groups made up of citizens free to press their own agenda within the limitations of lawful order.

In Western thought, economic modernization includes the development of the industrial and technological base but cannot be reduced to simple advances along these fronts. It is marked by growth, an increasingly specialized division of labor (with a global or international dimension), free market exchange, and the development of a cash economy. Modernization thought in the West also offers a particular view of *homo economicus*--with the focus on psychological traits addressing the relationship between motivation and entrepreneurial achievement (McClelland, 1961). In material terms, however, the linchpin of economic modernization is productive investment. Rostow (1964) holds that necessary capital for investment may come through taxation or confiscation; from organizations such as a stock market, banks and other lenders, and government securities; from international trade, with exports generating the foreign exchange to pay for imported capital goods (technology, etc.) used for production; and from foreign investment (private, governmental, or multilateral) resulting in the improvement of the infrastructure, the manufacturing base, or other forms of productive assets.

So (1990: 52-59, 85-87) has argued for the existence of two phases in modernization thought in the United States and the West. During the first or classical phase (roughly the 1950s and 1960s) modernization was presented as an irreversible, progressive, and lengthy process that assumed the Westernization of nation, society, and state. However, such attempts to explain and guide development quickly drew critical fire. The evolutionary thrust of a unidirectional and phased development in modernization thought was transparently one-dimensional. Put clearly, it appeared that from no matter where in its history a country might "take off," it would "land" in a Western European or U.S. airport.

This view not only appears somewhat chauvinistic but ignores the reality of development, especially in East Asia in the five decades following World War II. Despite "traditional" forms of culture, Japan and the "four dragons" (Singapore, Hong Kong, Taiwan, and the Republic of Korea) in this region showed remarkable industrial and technological growth, especially through the development of large export sectors. As to the contention that political democracy and market economies necessarily co-exist in history, the "dragons" to varying degrees relied on bureaucratic and authoritarian regimes, with Taiwan and the Republic of Korea resorting to martial force to quell political dissent, trade unions, Western-style individual liberties, and other expressions of the social contract. Contrary to the U.S. model, these nations did not follow the road of military Keynesianism and spent relatively little on warfare capacity. (As an aside, it might be noted that the Republic of South Africa was, by the standards of modernization, the most developed country on the African continent despite three centuries of racial politics that--until May 1994-- preserved democracy only for those of white European descent.) Thus the link between market development and Western democracy is far from absolute.

Given such problematics, the second phase of modernization theory, the modernization of modernization, sought to modify the more ideologized assumptions of its progenitor. Wong (1988) has argued that traditional aspects of Chinese commercial enterprises in Hong Kong seem to violate many

Western rules of business but are successful in the sense of development. The family unit, often closed to outsiders, practices nepotism, discourages external ownership by those not in the family, and is given to a form of highly controlled paternalism that shapes industrial relations. The workplace becomes a family (a common description more rhetorical than real in the United States), thus discouraging forms of disloyalty ranging from union organizing to the politics of class.

On the political side, new modernization thought may argue that economic development is a necessary but not sufficient condition for democracy. Huntington (1984) so argues, noting further that democracy (as in the case of Japan) may be imposed from the outside. However, he holds to the importance of market economies and the emergence of an independent and entrepreneurial bourgeoisie to facilitate "political development." Also of interest is the argument that democracy is often an evolutionary (as opposed to revolutionary) top-down process, resulting from the rituals of negotiations among the elite in a society.

Though the literature offers many examples, these cases demonstrate that the forces of reality and criticism moved the modernization agenda to embrace new positions. In the revision of modernization theory, tradition now emerged as a potential facilitator of development (as in East Asian familism, or in the case of new prodevelopment interpretations of Shinto in Japan or Islam in oil-rich countries). Historically founded case studies now supplanted the total reliance on generic typologies (such as achievement motivation) and grand theory. Development came to be seen as multidirectional, and not necessarily a carbon copy of the national economies of the world market core, while external and sometimes coercive forces (such as "democracy" by means of imperial expansion) were discovered.

Despite such modifications, modernization thought, research, and policy continued to face formidable academic and political criticism. Some of the critique assumed theoretical form in volumes of work from the dependency school, rooted in the work of such scholars as Paul Baran (see, for example, *The Political Economy of Growth* published in 1957) and Andre Gundar Frank (including his *Capitalism and Underdevelopment in Latin America,* published in 1969). Other exceptions to modernization bear the imprimatur of the world-system theory of Immanuel Wallerstein. Wallerstein and others argue the existence of a global (not national) capitalism, featuring systemic and asymmetrical ties among hierarchical world regions known as core, semiperiphery and periphery. Originating in the fifteenth century with the emergence of capitalist agriculture, the modern world system reflects political and cultural diversity but is linked by an economic organization that advances capital accumulation at the core. Taken as a whole, then, dependency and world-system thought is a critical response grounded in intellectual and political resistance to Adam Smith's laissez-faire economics and the assumption of a national and international division of labor on which it rests.

Although dependency and world-systems theory are also subject to criticism, the historical truth is that they are certainly not the basis for the ongoing transformational policies that link Poland's new order with Western nations and intergovernmental and transnational organizations. Hence, a thorough review of these traditions is somewhat tangential. Nevertheless, criticisms drawn from logic, the reality of development, and the critical traditions in the sociology of development are certainly relevant for explaining the most recent alterations and refinements of modernization thought.

To begin, modernization theory at the nexus is driven theoretically by values, not by material forces. Though much attention is given to the development of a market economy and the institutions of political democracy, it is routinely assumed that value constellations serve as either prime inhibitors or facilitators of modernization. The conception of values that drives modernization thought follows the sociology of Talcott Parsons and others who claim that generalized and shared criteria to evaluate social phenomena exist in culture. Hence values are something of a standard by which social and personality systems are linked and the objectives or ends of social action are selected by the actor. Throughout modernization thought, it is routinely assumed that values (whether those of tradition or those of "modern" social order) represent the engine of (or conversely, barriers to) development. In modernization thought, values cannot be reduced to the pluralist world of interests and veto nor to the materialist world of class and structure.

A critique of the centrality of values includes but goes beyond the usual dichotomy of cultural relativity and ethnocentrism. First, there is the question, Whose values are to drive the modernization process, and what is their specific content? The assumption that modernization rests on some form of transnational consensus implies the desirability of Western core values, whatever modifications one allows for indigenous transfiguration. The values argument sees behavior or action driven by an ideational world of shared meaning, ignoring the fact that societies often reflect considerable disagreement over values or that values may be in conflict. Although new modernization thought allows for the external imposition of values and the larger world of formal and popular culture, it does not address questions bearing on cultural forms of imperialism or hegemony. Above all, values discourse disregards structural forms of restraint. While crude structuralism may be overly deterministic, value consensus does not allow for the dialectic intersection of the world of phenomenology and that of realism.

In my view, modernization thought assumes a relativistic definition of development, not a relational one. Relativistic logic in development implies a common set of standards that determine how national economies can be ranked. The distinction between developed and developing countries commonly used by the Organisation for Economic Co-operation and Development, as well as by autonomous and related agencies of the United Nations (including the World Bank and the International Monetary Fund), is relativistic because it is the relative degree or absence of common indicators that serves as a basis for arraying nations into hierarchical categories. For example, the World Bank (1993: 238-324) arrays the 127 nations for which it has data into four categories measured in terms of gross national product (GNP) per capita: 1) low-income economies (N-40), 2) middle-income economies (N-43), 3) upper-middle-income economies (N-22) and 4) high-income economies (N-22). The basic indicators of development include: GNP-related measures, the rate of inflation, life expectancy, and adult illiteracy. Among the broader range of development indicators, the World Bank examines the growth and structure of development; value added in agriculture (with attention given to fertilizer consumption and average growth rate of food production per capita); summary measures of energy production and consumption; measures of manufacturing growth, earnings, and output; the growth and structure of consumption; trade; monetary holdings; official development assistance and various measures of debt and borrowing; and a more limited range of demographic, health, education, and other measures.

Relational conceptions of development differ in the emphasis on the dynamic, reciprocal, and often asymmetrical bonds and arrangements that tie national economies together. Whereas relativistic conceptions assume that developing economies are simply lacking the means to grow, relational analysis notes that national economies have not developed in hermetically sealed isolation. Some national economies (specifically feudal China and Japan) have attempted such a course. However, China in the eighteenth and early nineteenth century was opened for trade by the British, who quickly wearied of their negative balance of trade and initiated the opium trade, with its subsequent opium wars. Japan was forced to end its isolation when U.S. Commodore Matthew Perry opened the country to trade by gunboat.

More to the point, however, are the historical forces of colonization, the slave trade, imperialism, and unequal exchange in trade, with the price of finished goods from richer countries increasing in trade value at a faster rate than the unfinished materials and resources from poorer ones. These forces buttress the argument that the development of powerful national economies has benefited historically by the drawing of resources, both human and natural, from the bottom. The vast majority of the World Bank's low-income economies have a long history of colonization. In terms of imagery, it is one thing to argue that nations develop by finding their most productive niche in the international division of labor. It is quite another to view that division of labor as a barrier to, rather than a facilitator of, authentic development.

In sum, the British and other European colonial powers left a legacy of Western institutions and class relations when they were forced to yield political independence to their former possessions. Of greater importance today are the new forms of market and financial dependence still trapping those in the southern hemisphere in the new states of the twentieth century. The debt crisis is a case in point. From the relativistic view of development, nations wishing to modernize must borrow the capital and pay the debt through more productive economies and enhanced export earnings. From the relational view, debt ensures absorption into the world market order, ties up export earnings for debt service, and places the debtor at the mercy of large national economies who resort to protectionist measures when they experience recession.

Relational logic paints a darker portrait of global inequality, rendering it structural, relatively intractable, and regressive. While specific developing nations and some world regions have done better than others, the overall profile of the economic gap between rich and poor has widened during the era of modernization. Drawing from the United Nations Development Programme report of 1992 (pp. 34-47 passim), in 1960 the poorest 20 percent of the world's countries received 2.3 percent of global income and the richest 20 percent received 70.2 percent. In 1989, corresponding percentages were 1.4 percent for the poorest and 82.7 percent for the richest. Expressed another way, the ratio of the richest fifth of countries to the poorest fifth increased from 30-1 in 1960 to 59-1 in 1989. Such disparate figures are still tragically misleading, however, as they reflect the average or per capita incomes of whole countries. Incomes within countries are of course not distributed equally. When national income disparities are taken into account, the situation worsens dramatically. Looking at the world's people instead of the world's countries, the bottom 20 percent had a per capita income of $163 U.S.D. in 1988. The richest 20 percent had a per capita income of $22,808 U.S.D. Thus, the real ratio of richest to poorest people in 1988 was 140 to 1. The widening economic gaps between rich and poor over three decades (the 1960s through the 1980s) was evidenced in other measures such as trade, commercial bank lending, domestic investment, and domestic savings. One should not draw too much on a single measure, but in financial terms, foreign private investment (into richest countries versus poorest countries) was the single exception to the widening gap--holding steady at 21 to 1. As many modernization advocates inside poorer countries see this source of capital as crucial to developmental take off, one must conclude that (1) foreign investment continues to be pumped into rich-nation economies, and (2) even the absence of a growing disparity in this vital measure over three decades was not sufficient to halt continuing global pauperization.

On the more positive side, we find a narrowing disparity in certain measures of human development. The North-South gap in life expectancy decreased dramatically from 22.8 years in 1960 to 11.7 years in 1990. The corresponding infant mortality gap per 1,000 live births dropped from 123 to 61; the child mortality gap, from 187 to 94. There were corresponding gains in adult literacy, nutrition, and access to safe water. However, the gap widened when measured by mean years of schooling, tertiary education, scientists, and technicians per 1,000 people and other indicators. Whether expressed, then, in terms of product, income, or people, whether by measures of capital investment or human capital formation, the problem is a familiar one. The dynamics of international capital flows, trade, technology, and the labor market appear more apt to facilitate capital accumulation than poor nation modernization. Once again, we are reminded of the differences between growth and distribution.

Be all this as it may, the issue before us is not the development (or underdevelopment) of the periphery, but--given the momentous events of 1989 to 1991--the fall of the former command economies of the Soviet bloc countries in general and Poland in particular. The strategies and tactics of Polish development remain those of Western modernization, but it is a form of modernization that bears the imprint of the specific historical conditions of the region. With this in mind, it is now possible to construct a brief sensitizing argument. The special nature of the modernization crisis in postwar Poland is rooted in distinctive yet systemically related formations often overlapping in time. Hence, the modernization agenda and the nature of modernization thought in Poland must be differentiated from parallel problematics involving North-South global relations.

The first form of modernization crisis seizing Poland was rooted in a Soviet-style model of heavy industrialization that, while by no means destroying Polish agriculture or the independent Polish peasant, did move the country in the direction of becoming a giant factory. The crisis at this level emerged as the East bloc became largely isolated from the technological revolution (especially in information and communication) controlled by the national economies of the core. Attempts to trade with the West were compromised by ideology and national security concerns on both sides, with heavy state investment by the U.S.S.R., Czechoslovakia, and Poland on military capacity. Hence the bloc sought to retain military parity in the context of domestic economic decline.

Later decisions on the part of the Polish (as other) party elites only pushed the modernization crisis to a higher stage. Debt incurred in the name of development, dependency on new export industry in the context of Western market protectionism, and new policies threatening the closure of inefficient heavy industries (including shipbuilding) invited the crystallization of a social movement of broad-based resistance. (See chapters 1 and 2 in this volume). Martial law brought only a reprieve to the old regime, which continued its policies of market gradualism and heavy borrowing with no redeeming improvements in the balance of trade. However, the Polish modernization crisis was to reach its highest form in the early 1990s--with the institutionalization of policies of shock therapy based more on dramatics and ideology than on grounded economic policy. Poland became a laboratory for Darwinian remedies that had no record of trial in an industrial state.

PHASE III MODERNIZATION: THE CASE OF POLAND

The contours of the modernization crisis have not been lost on intergovernmental and transnational organizations or on those who hold the reins of state power, whatever the measure of their development. Dissent from the periphery has often been dismissed as impassioned rhetoric from newly decolonized states. However, widening disparities in wealth and income, the abysmal truth of absolute poverty, the massive growth in debt intended to finance modernization; these and a myriad of other warnings cannot be so casually dismissed. Ironically, it is the developed world's own penchant for data collection and its predilection for quantifying progress that now confronts those in command of the knowledge and information age. The indicators of global inequality are real enough, and the precipitous decline of living standards in the former Soviet bloc only provides further grounds for a critique of modernization thought, old and new, with its reliance on privatization, capital flows, free trade, and other dimensions of newly constructed laissez-faire. It may be possible to evade both history and responsibility and to deny more critical theory. But it is impossible to escape the consequences of a world in crisis.

What we shall term the crisis of Phase III modernization reflects an ongoing struggle to introduce human forms of development--as a means of moderating the social inequality associated with the growth imperative of the market economy. This permutation of modernization thought will be increasingly rooted in the principle that an unrestricted market economy will work to the advantage of those nations and classes that understand its forces and have the power to control events, while largely ignoring distribution and sustainability as alternative models of "progress."

As an example of examples, we turn to the United Nations Development Programme, which issued its first Human Development Report in 1990. While the focus of this report was on the states of the periphery, later reports began to address the new problems of Eastern European societies. The argument to be advanced here is that the still fledgling attempts to define and implement human development will be driven dramatically by events in Eastern Europe. As the modernization crisis intensifies, theory and rhetoric will reflect increasingly the dilemma of the human condition. In short, the rejection of Darwinian models of privatization in the former East Bloc will impel a reassessment of both the strategies and tactics of development. We should not be overcome with starry-eyed idealism, however. At this stage, it is arguable that the reconfiguration of modernization is more reform than synthesis. The following quotation is taken from the United Nations Development Programme (UNDP).

Human development is thus a broad and comprehensive concept. It covers all human choices in all societies in all stages of development. It broadens the development dialogue from a discussion of mere means [GNP growth] to a discussion of the ultimate ends. It is *as concerned with the generation of economic growth* [italics added] as with its distribution, as concerned with basic needs as with the entire spectrum of human aspirations, as concerned with the human dilemmas of the North as with the human deprivation in the South. The concept of human development does not start with any predetermined model. (UNDP, 1992: 2)

This last comment is arguable. The UNDP reports of 1990 and 1991 both stressed that the root causes of human deprivation are to be found in the national policies and institutional structures of the developing countries - reducing the role and responsibility of the developed world to that of interested bystander. But let the words speak for themselves: "Competitive markets are the best guarantee for efficient production. But these markets must be open to all the people. They require a skillfully crafted regulatory framework. And they must be supplemented by judicious social policy action" (UNDP, 1992: 1). There can be little doubt that this is the modernization imperative that we have described above, refitted to address the problem of a "human face."

As these exemplars demonstrate, the modernization paradigm covers a range of explanatory and ideological attempts drawn from economics, political science, sociology, and psychology. Its assumptions and assertions have been strongly criticized and refined in the course of its post-World War II existence. For now, we shall focus on a given. Modernization, whether in the form of organizational policy, practice, or ideology, drives the transnational relations of the world market order. To comprehend this is a beginning point for examining the mission and behavior of transnational and intergovernmental organizations within the developed world--and the specific nature of their relations with the new republic of Poland. However, the scale and rate of pauperization in this and other former party/states can be expected to force new thinking on human development. As we shall see in due course, it remains to be seen whether the new development focus will emerge as real or remain rhetorical. To assess future prospects for Poland and the new democracies of Eastern and Central Europe, it is essential to place events in a transnational context.

OECD: PARTNERS IN TRANSITION

The Organisation for Economic Co-operation and Development, established in 1960, is intergovernmental in structure and membership. It consists of twenty-four market democracies and can be conceived as a sister institution to the World Bank. Its policy directives are to "achieve the highest sustainable economic growth and employment; contribute to economic and social welfare throughout the OECD area; stimulate and harmonize its Members' efforts in favor of developing countries; [and] contribute to the expansion of world trade on a multilateral, nondiscriminatory basis ("OECD Work on Economic Reform," undated: 1). OECD-sponsored discourse, consultation, and programs constitute only one exemplar of modernization. For example, the United Nations Economic Commission for Europe, established in 1947 to assist in the reconstruction of Europe, also largely conceives of development as bound to the modernization framework.

The OECD's organizational history is rooted in the events of postwar Europe. The U.S. Marshall Fund provided the financial support for the Organisation for European Economic Co-operation (OEEC), dedicated in turn to the rebuilding of the European market economies. OECD is the successor organization of the old OEEC, and its enlarged mandate includes facilitating cooperation, primarily among the more powerful Western economies and Japan (though Turkey is also affiliated). A prime organizational imperative is the compilation of reliable data to assess international economic interactive trends and international policy interactions.

The organizational duties of OECD provide some insight into its priorities. By means of its committees, secretriat, and autonomous agencies, the organization addresses economic, financial and trade policies; energy (including nuclear) issues; science, technology and industry; public management; environmental policy; and social affairs, labor, and education. Within the scope of relations with nonmember countries, the OECD agenda for Eastern Europe in the early 1990s was the responsibility of the Centre for Co-operation with European Economies in Transition (CCEET). At the Houston Economic Summit in July of 1990, the heads of state for the G-7 (the major Western industrial powers and Japan) requested that the four leading Western development organizations study the Soviet economy with a view toward establishing policy to guide economic assistance and other support. This mandate was to be carried out by the World Bank, the International Monetary Fund, the European Bank for Reconstruction and Development, and OECD. The aforementioned Centre for Co-operation with European Economies in Transition headed up the effort for OECD, but its broader mission addressed the range of Central and Eastern European privatization.

The CCEET program is heavily geared toward the provision of technical expertise. However, the range of services to assist the European transition reveals a familiar if implicit design. For OECD, the modernization of Eastern Europe is conceived in terms of developing the technical expertise and institutions of a market-oriented economy. The subject matter includes economic development and structural adjustment based on the "successful experiences of industrial or newly industrialized countries ("OECD Work on Economic Reform," undated: 6)." Other concerns addressed by the organization's technical staff include competition (as embodied in law, antimonopoly enforcement); labor market (focus on such issues as flexibility, entrepreneurial capacity, training, solving labor disputes); banking and financial systems (the efficient allocation of resources to the free enterprise sector); taxation; trade liberalization; foreign direct investment; industrial privatization and restructuring (including the role of small and medium-sized enterprises in economic development); agriculture; energy; and finally, education and environmental initiatives.

A few orienting observations can be made about OECD and CCEET initiatives, which are borne out by the record, by the organization's literature, and by interviews with officials and consultants. First, the agenda is clearly committed to the economic side of market development, with human development issues, such as education and the environment, ranking well toward the bottom of the list, literally and in terms of budgetary priorities. (See, for example, OECD, 1991c.) Human development is thus more or less organizational ideology, with the United States (at least during the Reagan and Bush administrations) the prime opponent to such concerns as "green development."

Opposition to policies of structural internalization of environmental costs may have begun to weaken somewhat in Western circles. However, the imbalance remains. The contradiction is a foreboding one. Given the massive problems of pollution throughout Eastern and Central Europe, with the enormous toll on environmental health, the failure to internalize the human and economic costs in development plans can prove to be a fateful error. For example, industrial pollution not only destroys human health but degrades the potential for cleaner industries such as tourism. It is not simply Western organizations that are at fault. Modernization ideology and policy also drove the command economies of the former East bloc and new regimes have yet to develop new thinking.

Returning to initiatives in Eastern Europe, OECD established its Partners in Transition program in addition to the activities already launched under the auspices of its CCEET. The program was "specifically designed for those countries that have demonstrated a resolute commitment to a rapid transition to a market economy and to pluralistic democracy and have expressed the wish to entertain special links with the OECD" (OECD, 1991b: 2). Poland was one of three countries (together with Hungary and the former Czech and Slovak Federal Republic) deemed to be most advanced with regard to market development and finding their place in the system of world trade. Consistent with the description of OECD initiatives above, the prime imperative of Partners in Transition was the facilitation of market development. However, the Partners in Transition program did allow for periodic reviews of sectorial issues--including such human development concerns as social policy, education, and the environment. It is to these questions that we now turn.

The Partners in Transition Program should not be viewed in isolation. In the aftermath of the Round Table negotiations, the new Polish leadership began a concerted campaign to forge new political connections with the Bretton Woods organizations (specifically the World Bank and the IMF), the European Union, OECD, and the Council of Europe. The Council of Europe connection indicated the Polish interest in building Western-style institutions of civil society. Warsaw desired an architecture for the integration of the country into the New Europe and the world market system, the restructuring of the economy toward sectors of "comparative advantage"--and the realization of such objectives posthaste. From the perspective of Warsaw, Partners in Transition represented a first-stage legitimacy for its efforts at modernization. From the OECD perspective, this entry-level arrangement would conceivably lead to full membership. As noted in its "Memorandum of Understanding" with the three affected governments, reviews conducted by OECD might be shared with the IMF, the World Bank, and other representatives (1991c: 6).

More perceptive officials at OECD headquarters in Paris know the Polish situation well enough to be wary of a simple cloning approach that ignored the egalitarian values in Poland. The risk as seen from inside the organization was that the concentration of sacrifice and pain among weaker and poorer Poles would lead to social opposition, thus threatening the reform process. The same perceptive voices spoke of the need for educational reforms, a social safety net, and strong environmental safeguards. Also recognized was the need for a new "natural" market for Eastern Europe with the decline of COMECON, in view of the tendency in the European Union and other developed economies to protect their own markets despite the rhetoric of free trade.

However frank such views (clearly consistent with the reality of the international division of labor), there is often a chasm between the tacit understandings of officials and experts and the policies of organizations. It is not so much the organizational culture of development organizations that requires reexamination in the light of human development imperatives; it is rather the structurally rooted consistency of the policies that extend across organizational boundary lines. These policies reflect the modernization imperative defined above. Thus, as one OECD consultant noted, external assistance will not be important in driving environmentally sound development. Hence, affected countries must take the initiative on such issues. The goal of sustainable development, although ultimately essential (and included in OECD literature) thus confronts the hard reality of economism.

Representative of OECD initiatives in the region as of the early 1990s was the recurring interest in service sector development. Structural adjustments in this sector were specifically defined as tied to the development of telecommunications. Needless to say, Western organizations would supply much of the technology and the technicians, with a joint venture on the manufacturing of switches (involving Spain, France, and Germany) approved by Warsaw. U.S. West was also involved in bringing a mobile telephone capacity. Although these early initiatives emphasized the importance of international, organizational, and industrial telecommunications, the provision of personal telephones to those who could afford installation and service fees was deemed paramount to the success of this form of modernization.

While the improvement of telecommunications is certainly not an evil unto itself, there is a relational side to OECD and other Western attempts to build the service sector of the Polish and other Eastern European economies. From the Western view, the underdevelopment of the service sector is tied with the overdevelopment of the heavy manufacturing sector. It is true enough that much heavy industry in Poland is technologically marginal and inefficient and that it remains a source of massive environmental degradation. It is also true that heavy manufacturing has been that sector reflecting a level of state involvement ideologically anathema to the United States--and to those organizations within which it is influential. However, that form of big-bang modernization rooted in catastrophic deindustrialization had--as of 1994--buried Poland in a wave of unemployment. Even for the powerful economy of the United States, deindustrialization in the 1970s and 1980s--with a corresponding shift toward service sector growth--had led to structural pauperization in the labor force, as service sector employment offered less compensation in the form of both wages and benefits.

Of particular relevance for conceptions of modernization more greatly influenced by questions of human development is an idea found in the deconstruction of the discourse of educational reform. Education in modernization thought is fundamental to human capital formation; it is a pillar of human development as seen in both United Nations Development Programme and World Bank initiatives. However, the question before us is: What is education? Or, more specifically, What is education for the new Polish order? A broad reading of OECD initiatives in the early 1990s reveals a number of thematic areas, all of which are held together by a common assumption: education should be restructured to reflect the needs of the emerging market economy.

Such approaches are not novel of course; nor are they confined to Central and Eastern Europe in the present era. In the 1980s, a massive restructuring of U.S. higher education brought the decline of the liberal arts and a massive growth in business, accounting, computer science, technology and applied courses of study in four-year institutions. Such educational changes were supposedly responses to market demand (meaning simply that students wanted jobs and these skills were supposed to pay off). Despite such marketization, graduates continued to face a tighter job market with resulting underemployment. The restructuring problem thus proved to have less to do with the development of marketable skills and more to do with uncontrolled market forces. These included megamergers, the growth of the secondary labor market, technological displacement of workers, the globalization of the economy, the rise of the service sector, and capital flight, all of which led to a well-documented increase in inequality and the further erosion of the middle class in the richest market economy on earth. Should such social problems in the United States (and other wealthier nations) be frankly shared with the new democracies, new conceptions and policies of development might be forthcoming.

An overriding Western theme in the transformation of education centers on the development of entrepreneurial skills. In an OECD-sponsored Conference on Education and the Economy in Central and Eastern Europe (June 29-July 1, 1992), a workshop on entrepreneurship was led by the Polish delegation. The conception of entrepreneurialism is revealing.

Narrowly interpreted, entrepreneurship is that body of skill and knowledge required in business activities. As practised in an education setting, this typically manifests itself in groups of students, either within the curriculum or on an extra-curricular basis, who are setting up and running a real or a simulated business. More broadly interpreted, entrepreneurship embodies the attributes, qualities and abilities which encompass *creativity, powers of taking and exercising responsibility, the ability to solve problems, to learn, to take initiatives, and to be flexible, adaptable, active purposeful and self-confident.* In all the post-communist societies, there is hardly any tradition of education and training for entrepreneurship in either its narrower or broader sense [italics added]. (OECD 1992a: 8)

This excerpt is not an official OECD policy statement, but it does demonstrate the distressing elasticity of terms during periods of ideological absolutism. To argue that such values alone comprise entrepreneurialism ignores the material side of development. There has indeed been a dramatic shift in the overt celebration of the individual and personal freedom in Poland, and this is evidenced in a new axiology. However, the key to entrepreneurialism is not a simple revolution in values, but the availability of venture capital. Venture capital in turn introduces the range of dependency issues considered above.

On the important question of social responsibility, entrepreneurs seeking profit maximization exist in a particular relation, both to their employees and to society. Entrepreneurialism may thrive under conditions of cheap labor, leveraged capital to control assets, minimal taxes, and noninterference. Entrepreneurialism is often opportunistic even in developed market economies, but in Poland and other former East bloc countries these "virtues" have often taken the form of buying and selling in the black or gray as well as legitimate markets. Such activities may generate profit and consumption, but do not necessarily build a new productive base while they are allowing for the evasion of taxes in a context of political underdevelopment.

A permutation of the entrepreneurial theme is familiar. A principle of the early modernization studies was that the growth of markets and entrepreneurialism were inextricably linked to the political side of development. In *Innovation and Employment*, a newsletter published jointly by the OECD and the Commission of the European Communities, we find the following: "Small and medium-sized business owners are the potential middle class of the formerly Communist countries and one of the most important pillars of a properly functioning democracy" (Nov. 1991: 1). Democracy (here, as in many discussions) is left undefined--which is curious, given that this is one of the most abused terms in political history. However, taking the Western representative model on face, it is arguable that the supposed invariate relationship between market freedom and political freedom is more ideological than real. (See the earlier discussion of East Asian and South African development.)

A Polish representative to the same Conference on Education and the Economy, while not offering an official OECD view, also took up the agenda in a discussion of "orienting education and training to stimulate entrepreneurship" (1992b: 22-23). The following excerpts are instructive:

1. The promotion of individualistic-competitive values, opposing populism and developing an elitist approach is indispensable for stimulating the spirit of entrepreneurship (OECD, 1992B: 22-23). Individualised programmes for talented students will pave the way for creating future professional and intellectual elites. . .

2. The system of (Polish) education, irrespective of the level of teaching and specialisation should be adapted to future professional careers. Meanwhile, it is difficult to find today any relationship between the subject taught and a future job, either in textbooks or in the mode of teaching.

3. It will not be an easy task to implant a conviction that work is the highest good rather than a necessary evil. Nobody can doubt, however, that the *present conditions are very favourable*. [Italics added].Unemployment is growing rapidly, personal incomes are differentiated on an unprecedented scale, pay preferences are clearly given to educated, enterprising or innovative persons, and finally high incomes can be obtained in occupations and specialisations in great demand during the transition to a market economy.

4. The State's obligation to provide free education should be restricted to primary and secondary education.

The "logic" here is that modernization favors the talented--who, spurred by the mounting fear of unemployment, will seek their own self-interest in a way that automatically builds a sound economic base. Not surprisingly, there is no evidence cited to support this statement of Darwinian faith. Unemployment in Poland at the time of this conference (1992) had gone from 1/2 of 1 percent to approximately 12 percent in less than three years. (A year later, conservative statistics put the rate at 15 to 16 percent.) Industrial production had dropped by May 1992 to 57.5 percent of its 1989 level. The argument that unemployment and industrial decline favor modernization assumes that it is necessary to destroy the economy in order to save it.

A far softer version of entrepreneurialism can also be discerned in the literature from development conferences sponsored by the OECD. In a local development strategies session sponsored jointly with the John F. Kennedy School of Government at Harvard, a quite different model of entrepreneurialism (the case of Finland) demonstrated the integration of public and private sector initiatives on the promotion of innovation (OECD, 1991b). In Finland, communities and municipalities have a liaison officer to help entrepreneurs through the bureaucracy, and every county provides organizational support to facilitate export, the training of managers, and the adaptation of new technology. Training seminars on management skills, production, financial support, and trade attract some 10,000 entrepreneurs yearly. Central government regionalized offices offer expert consultants to assist companies in technological upgrades, marketing, and other business areas. There is an entrepreneurial department organized under the National Ministry of Trade and Industry.

One of the more intriguing aspects of the Finnish approach deals with financing and risk financing. Finland features a highly developed local banking system founded historically on a dual system of cooperative banks and those owned on a private basis. Branches of larger merchant banks are also located in municipalities and cities. As a purely local banking system cannot assume high levels of risk, legislation prohibits such lending practices for smaller banks. Finland relies on such authorities as the State Guarantee Institutes to back up local bank loans, and the Regional Development Fund of Finland, which is empowered to make riskier loans. By the end of the 1980s, the fund was assisting some 700 to 900 new enterprises yearly. Hence, risk is apportioned among entrepreneurs, banks, and government.

What emerges from the OECD literature is the stark contrast between the vision of privatization known as shock therapy and the far milder public-private initiatives in OECD countries with strong social democratic traditions. Hence entrepreneurialism has a considerable variety of implications and meanings when placed in more specific contexts. However, vast differences exist in terms of the stage of development between established market economies and those of Eastern and Central Europe (including Poland). Simply exhorting the unemployed to become entrepreneurs or workers to work harder in a draconian vortex of crisis is an evasion of economic history.

It is not simply that problems exist in the establishment of the skills required of actors in the market economy, or in the growth and development of financial and banking systems and the sharing of risks. It is also noted that an infrastructural deficit exists in telecommunications and transportation, and that the old centralized division of labor was tied in great measure to giant plants scattered throughout the entire East bloc region. Such arrangements not only resulted in problems of distance and delivery, they ensured that a breakdown in one element would reverberate throughout an interdependent system. The scope of such problems appear to be beyond the rhetoric of shock therapy or even the provision of public sector expertise. From a human development perspective, the role of education is vital. However, in the OECD view of the role of education in the Polish transformation, the larger issue of human development often appears to give way to that of a narrowly conceived human capital formation, addressing the specific labor force skills required to power the market economy. The unfortunate dilemma here is that in a market economy, taxes based on individual and corporate incomes are crucial to the funding of the education, science, technology, and research related to human capital formation.

OECD literature on education has taken the view that as "education is not homogeneous, the role of the state will differ from one level of education to the next" (1992b: 6). In this view, the state should finance primary and secondary education, either directly or through the private sector. With respect to vocational and technical education, government intervention and financing should be more limited, with the costs of skill-specific training borne by enterprises and taking the form of the European apprenticeship system. The question for Poland, one which is not often addressed by Western advisors, is how declining enterprises are to take over this responsibility from a state that is suffering through mounting revenue deficits.

One troubling aspect of organizational ideology, certainly not confined to the OECD, centers on the assumption that Eastern and Central European states in fiscal crisis "overspend on income maintenance programmes which do not add much value to human capital, and underspend on education, science, technology and research, which are vital to human capital formation. Adjusting the structure of cash benefits and improving targeting will become increasingly important to avoid further reductions in the provision of social services such as education and training" (OECD 1992b: 7).

Stated simply, the new regimes in the region are being asked to trade off meager income maintenance (a reactive response to the present crisis) against the considerations of human capital formation. With a significant segment of the population locked in the vise of short-term survival needs, the long term may not be a viable humanitarian or political option. The tendency to reify the economy so that the relation between economy and society is made to disappear is a common feature of the ideology of modernization. Viewed from the perspective of the legions of newly pauperized and marginalized Poles, the premise that unequally shared misery will ultimately contribute to the greater good appears not only unproven, but cruel and unjust. The market may or may not be said to have a human face, but misery always does.

Further considered, the ideology of modernization--perhaps quite inadvertently--reproduces diversionary forms of victim blaming. This is not to deny the need for internal changes in economy, polity, and society, but to say that the larger responsibilities of the international community are often ignored when internal features of crisis are overemphasized. To illustrate, a common refrain within the modernization agenda for new states targets the importance of efficiency. With regard to human capital formation, OECD literature notes: "In the majority of CEE countries, a significant amount of resources are wasted in the provision of education and training services because technical processes are ineffective and/or management methods inadequate. Inefficiencies are pervasive throughout the system, and resources do not achieve the desired result" (1992b: 8-9).

In a design calling for the restructuring of Polish education to facilitate human capital formation, OECD cites as a "striking example" of inefficiency the "extremely low" student-teacher ratios (standing at 18-1 for primary and secondary education in Poland). At the higher education level, inefficiencies are identified in the "very large network of small teaching and research institutions," and the view of efficiency conversely is one of "consolidating the number of institutions" (Ibid). Whereas it may be useful to tighten networks and examine fragmented organizational structures, progress is being defined here in terms of increased class size and larger departments. This view may lead to measures that save money, but it contradicts pedagogical studies that demonstrate a clear relationship between smaller classes and better-paid teachers on the one hand and earnings of students on the other. (OECD does recognize as problematic the "low salaries of teachers" in Eastern and Central Europe.)

Robert Reich, former Harvard political economist and Secretary of Labor under the Clinton administration, has taken a very different view of optimal student-teacher ratios:

Researchers have found that schools with smaller classes and better-paid teachers produce young people who command higher salaries once they join the work force. David Card and Alan Krueger, researchers at Princeton University, studied the education and incomes of a million men born from 1920 to 1949 who attended the public schools. They found that even within the same socio-economic group, higher lifetime earnings correlate with smaller class size and better paid-teachers. The extra tax revenues generated by these higher lifetime incomes alone would finance the smaller classes and better paid teachers. (cited in Perdue, 1993b: 116)

Ultimately, then, the ability to finance education in a market system rests with the will to tax concentrated wealth and with the tax-paying capacity that rises with the skill levels of workers, though wage policies to counteract the power of employers represent the other side of the relation. Poland's small class sizes in education could ultimately pay dividends, if the nation receives the international financial assistance necessary to weather the larger fiscal crisis. The insistence that this Polish advantage be compromised as a condition for acceptance in the organizational world of transnational and intergovernmental market managers is a short-term expedient, but a long-term contradiction. The challenge is how to maintain low student-teacher ratios while improving the pay of teachers in the interest of authentic long-term development.

OECD worried that the Polish state as of 1992 had moved the direct responsibility for kindergarten education to the local level, creating a crisis in local funding, as such governments are limited in their powers to raise revenues. The OECD position was that local governments might serve as local educational agents of the center, which would remain the main source of funding. This view does offer a creative synthesis in lieu of the dichotomy of overcentralization on the one hand and fragmentation on the other (1992b: 9). However, moving the responsibility for early childhood education was not a feature of Polish democratization, but a response to the fiscal crisis of the State. This form of passing on the funding responsibility for education--from the center to the communities--is another clear and present threat to the Polish future.

Another threat to what has been traditionally excellent in Poland is evidenced in the crude economism of much modernization thought. For example: "In higher education, resources continue to be channelled to programmes with little relevance to the needs of a market economy, and the real priorities are not taken into account. Over time, a greater proportion of public funding should shift towards demand driven formulae which encourage greater responsiveness to the needs of enterprises and individuals" (OECD, 1992b: 10). Such new priorities, ranging from more classes in business economics and management to technology and the substitution of short-cycle courses in technician training for long-term university tutelage, would simply replace the bearers of the massive Polish intellectual and cultural traditions with new technocrats. Technological and managerial skills certainly have their place, but when conceived and implemented in a narrow fashion, they are an exercise in planned labor force obsolescence at the professional level.

One of the clearest illustrations of the ideology of modernization is found in its unilinear and teleological assumptions about social change. The imagery of progressive change toward a historical endpoint is redundant in OECD and other development literature--with Poland (as the new democracies of Eastern and Central Europe) seen to be moving through phases of transition or transformation. An exemplar of this imagery is evidenced in a paper presented at an OECD-organized conference in Warsaw (October 1993). In it, Oden schematizes the transition to a market economy as movement from the "dismantling of central planning: restructuring and privatisation," to the "development of market relations: restructuring to competitive competence," and finally to "transformation and modernisation: competitive competence to competitive advantage" (Oden, 1993: 15). While this view of phases is subdivided into many categories, the first three dimensions of this imagery of the Polish transition will be sufficient to make the point.

Oden presents a view of a gradually improving macroeconomic environment. Early on there are to be expected sharp declines in output and employment, price inflation, and productivity; moving in tandem with an austere fiscal and monetary policy. At a second level, the market is assumed to take hold and there is interim improvement. And finally, output and employment are to begin growing, relative prices are to reflect market forces, productivity is to be enhanced by technical change, and austere fiscal and monetary constraints can be loosed. A similar progression is seen in capital markets--from scarce markets then to thin and unstable ones, and finally to availability for "successful firms and new entrants"--and in labor, from large-scale displacement, then to a slowing rate of unemployment, and finally to new employment with wages supposedly linked to productivity and adaptability to new technology and work organization (Oden, 1993: 15).

Earlier, reference was made to the rather curious expectation that Eastern and Central Europe were supposed to build capitalism without the capital. Consider for a moment Rostow's argument described earlier that successful modernization rests on productive investment. What are the sources of productive investment to be for Poland? Taxation--the traditional bane of entrepreneurialism? Confiscation? This was the oppressive method of the Stalinist modernization model. Stock markets, banks, and lenders? These presuppose existing capital reserves. Trade? The issue here is barriers such as the E.U.'s "Farmer's Wall." Foreign investment? While making some small impact in Poland at this writing, private investment tends to follow success and stability. A related point is that almost 95 percent of global commercial lending is confined to the upper 20 percent of national economies (UNDP, 1992: 36). This leaves governmental or multilateral sources of productive investment--and forces one to ask why the question of a Marshall Plan fashioned to support authentic development of Central and Eastern Europe has not been seriously entertained. (See chapter 14 in *Modernization Crisis* Perdue, 1995.)

UNESCO AND THE INSTITUTIONS OF CIVIL SOCIETY

Moving the discussion from economic to civil development provides us with another dimension of the wider transnational view. The United Nations Educational, Scientific and Cultural Organization (UNESCO) was founded in London on November 16, 1945. It was and is committed to the promotion of collaboration among member nations and nongovernmental organizations toward the ends of education, science, and culture. A specialized and related agency enjoying a functional relationship with the United Nations Organization, UNESCO is nevertheless autonomous. Although representing a wide variety of initiatives and values, the preamble of the founding convention for the creation of UNESCO declares that "wars are born in the spirit of man, and it is thus in the spirit of man that must be elevated the defenses of peace." Committed to human rights, intellectual and moral solidarity, and the understanding of customs, UNESCO offers insight into multicultural conceptions of freedom and democracy. The intellectual initiatives of the organization with regard to democracy building in Eastern and Central Europe provide some insight into the problematic of civil society as conceived in the West.

The crisis of civil society for the region in general and Poland in particular is often presented as a tertiary problem to be resolved more or less automatically with the successful construction of the market economy. This dimension of the ideology of modernization can be very misleading, as our critique has demonstrated. To be sure, the anticommunist wave in the region served to open the door to civil ideologies and movements to check the antidemocratic power of the party/state. However, the fall of such regimes is but a necessary condition for the establishment of authentic people's rule. The clear and present danger is that a new elite--given standing by still emerging hierarchical relations and operating in the context of systemic crisis--will not be restrained by the underdeveloped institutions of civil society.

Alain Touraine set the tone for a UNESCO-sponsored International Forum, "Culture and Democracy," held in Prague in September 1991, when he asked: "What do we celebrate today? The fall of authoritarian regimes or the victory of democracy?" (1991: 2). The two can easily be separated, as Touraine notes, because military and ideological mobilization against all forms of opposition to new regimes may be mounted in the name of liberation and independence. While it is certainly true at this juncture that Poland has not fallen prey to forms of nationalist reaction (as in the former Yugoslavia) or to a resurgence of Stalinism, the specter of crisis hangs heavy in the land. And while markets may not ensure mature and authentic forms of democracy, the shock of privatization represents a clear and present danger to the forms of novitiate democracy struggling to survive.

The challenge of democracy ultimately transcends the question of free choice in the political sphere. Instead, the project of democracy must be viewed in systemic and relational terms--political, economic, and sociocultural. The claims of political equality in a context of growing inequality in wealth and income is a problem for powerful market economies such as the United States, where the institutional arrangements of class are supported by the long power of tradition and tend to appear as part of the natural order of things. In Poland, new class formations represent unique forms of crisis.

Shock therapy modernization introduces two troubling possibilities for the immediate future. One concerns the historical schism between the new bourgeoisie and a culture of public responsibility. This gap may be even wider in Poland than elsewhere, where new conceptions of wealth building may encourage opportunism more than civic duty. The second corollary problem at the structural level is that new class formations--legitimated by the merited inequality assumed to drive modernization--will take root much more quickly than the moderating institutions of civil society. This is because the architects of modernization assume that democracy is a by-product of markets, and spend both energy and treasure accordingly. As wealth, income, and power are concentrated in a context of crisis, the temptations to use state power in the service of new formations of privilege may grow. Hence, the project of civil society is of vital interest to the future of the region.

The conceptualization of civil society is often an exercise in theoretical elasticity, rooted as it is in shifting explanations of the relations among economy, state, and society. For our purposes, we shall offer a reconstructed image formulated in the work of Antonio Gramsci (1971), who conceived of civil society as social formations occupying the terrain between the state and the sphere of economic production. This is the terrain of citizenship and personal liberty, which for Gramsci represented a sphere of illusion and ideological distortion. Possible institutional and organizational actors within the realm of civil society might include education, religion, national culture, and unions. Whether the contractual promise of civil society exists as something other than illusion is of course the essence of the debate and practice of democracy. It is for these reasons that the project of citizenship shall be qualified herein as authentic to the extent that such a sphere is free of domination by either economy or state--or more accurately, by the systemic relations between the two.

In exploring the problematic of authentic civil society, one necessarily encounters dilemmas born of the procedural prerequisites of democracy building. The strength (or perhaps more accurately, the legitimacy) of the democratic standing of the state may be found in such formal procedures as constitutions ensuring basic rights to personal liberties such as speech, religion, and so forth, as well as those manifestly designed to protect the person against the abuse of state power. Other formal procedures include guarantors of representation such as periodic elections and specified terms in office and various measures designed to ensure openness and accountability on the part of public officials. Of course, procedural safeguards are rooted in the underlying assumption of democracy that people can be trusted with political power and that from their midst will rise men and women of principle and trust who will safeguard the public interest.

In the aforementioned UNESCO conference, Claus Offe identified concerns of democracy building that are related in important ways to this discussion. He asks, "Who is to guard the constitution if it comes under stress and pressure. . . . if the outcomes, as left to the contingencies of competitive party politics and market forces, are seen as less favorable for at least some of the time by at least some portion of the people, and also if the initial hope and enthusiasm invested in the newly established democratic institutions should evaporate?" (1991: 5-6). To Offe's concern that nationalism is more a threat than guarantee (given the ancient dilemma of democracy, the tyranny of the majority) must be added the observation that a culture of democracy, however defined, cannot simply be called into existence by enacting procedures, identifying levels of political power, and establishing a system of checks and balances. All of these presuppose some investiture of faith and confidence, some embodiment of an active public trust, and some vigilance on the part of a knowing and organized citizenry. Such problems have not been resolved in many societies that claim centuries of experience with Western-style democratic institutions.

I share Offe's concern that the presence of trusted and charismatic leaders is also no guarantee of democracy. It is uncertain whether unusually dynamic leaders are going to emerge in every historical era, as it is uncertain whether charismatic leaders will defend constitutions or the broader fabric of democratic institutions. However, I would add that issues relating to character and high-mindedness (while of some importance) also work to reduce the structural questions of role expectations and performance to personal assessments that invite idiosyncratic judgments. Hence, one might narrowly question whether a president, prime minister, secretary general, or the like is good or competent or charismatic--as opposed to asking whether the more enduring structural relations involving state, society, and economy are truly democratic. It is such structural relations, and only secondarily questions of character, that shape the content and real expectations of the leadership role. Thus conceived, a *President* Walesa is of greater significance for formal democracy than a President *Walesa*. The role endures, while the person does not.

Offe (1991) also notes that "collective actors" have been relied upon in Western politics to offer some sort of stability and counterbalance to the quest for democracy. These are the familiar pluralist forces of civil society ranging from independent trade unions to leagues of farmers, from employers' organizations to professional associations, and so on. His argument that such formations were not strong in postcommunist societies might have been questioned in Poland when Solidarity and its allies were strong and vital. However, Offe must be said to be prescient in his skepticism, even if he did not mention the situation in Poland and thus ignored what appeared in 1991 to be Polish exceptionalism. Collective actors did unite under the banner of Solidarity for the purpose of resistance. However, Solidarity the party was not to survive as so credible a force, and its collective constituencies have little in the way of institutional memory.

There is a higher argument to be considered here, one that questions the pluralist conceptions of countervailing power that underlie most Western constructions of civil society and democracy building. Critically conceived, it is not within the procedural domain of the state and civil society that one finds the essence of democracy. In the event of massive concentration of real power in the sphere of economic production, the unidimensional construction of democracy as civil or political only denies the broader implications of the term. Elections may become mocking rituals in the context of unemployment and pauperization; a kind of cruel consolation prize for the marginalized. Argued thus, a standard of distributive justice (reflecting the imperatives of shared sacrifice and a minimum standard of need) is a necessary, if not sufficient, condition for the success of authentic institutions of civil society. Democracy cannot be confined to one sphere or another. It is the nature of the relations among economy, state, and society that demonstrates in real and practical terms whether democracy is collective empowerment or ideology, illusion and mystification.

Also at the UNESCO conference in Prague, Mihailo Markovic (1991) noted that the political culture of democracy requires political literacy on the part of citizens and that a part of that literacy requires exposure to opposing views. Building on this insight, we may uncover yet another dilemma of civil society and democracy building embodied in the historical nature of the Eastern European transformation. Opposition forces by definition come to embody the ideological antithesis of the existing order. The hardships of national struggle and the need for clarity in purpose facilitates dichotomous conceptions of black and white, good and evil. When, after a long period of difficult resistance, the old regime is swept away, the collective self-definition of opposing forces remains. Ideas that appear somehow related to the old order are suspect--as are those who might voice them.

In general philosophical terms, such ideological rigidity (on the popular level and on the part of successor regimes) can only reduce the realm of rational argumentation, solutions, and choices, and is hence antidemocratic. Ironically, the policies of older market democracies (especially those of Northern and, to a lesser degree, Western Europe) include a wide range of human development interventions institutionalized in the public sector. These are designed to mitigate the natural proclivities of the market toward the concentration of wealth and income. However, such public sector interventions (including Northern and Western European-style planning) came to be defined in some quarters of Poland as a residual of the old regime, and hence beyond the limits of legitimate discourse.

The early legitimation of privatization in Poland and elsewhere thus thrived in an internal atmosphere in which debates about social inequality could not flourish. However, it is crucial to note that the threat to authentically democratic discourse must be understood at both the internal and external levels. Internally, the utopian ideology of opposition movements more or less generally becomes the new ideology of order. With the old regime swept away, the rejection of its remaining cultural, psychological, and material imprints may correspondingly be generalized to other targets of convenience. In the Polish case, devotion to privatization became something of a new political loyalty test. At the external level, the policies of development banks, consultants, financial institutions, and private investors of the core economies (whether anticipated and intended or not) encouraged such views. In Poland, the new Solidarity government, desperate in the early 1990s to belong to the only order left standing, followed a path of extremist rejectionism of the old order. One hopeful sign of a stronger progressive opposition is found in the emergence of the labor party, where former Solidarity activists, pro-choice organizers, and democratic socialists may offer a reasoned critique of laissez-faire. At this writing, it remains to be seen whether the elections of September, 1993 will prove to be a step away from unidimensional ideology, and a means of enlarging authentic democratic discourse.

UNESCO documentation on the *problematique* of democracy also addresses the broader relational milieu that continue to plague nations that claim long democratic traditions. One of these is minority representation. Defined sociologically, the term minority is not about numbers, but rather about power. Now, for those whose first principle of democracy is majority rule, it may come as a surprise to find that there is often weakness, not strength, in numbers. Perhaps the prime example is the condition of women. Even Switzerland, long cited as an exemplar of markets and shared power, was very late in recognizing the right of women to vote.

In an overview of women's representation in the lower chambers of parliament, Drude Dahlerup (1991) noted that the recognized democracies were very different. Representation ranged from 2 percent in Japan, 6 percent in France, and 7 percent in the United States to 24 percent in Iceland, 33 percent in Denmark, 36 percent in Norway, 38 percent in Sweden and 39 percent in Finland. There are those (primarily in countries where women are dramatically underrepresented) who argue that representation should be based on competence, not gender. However, by this standard, American, French, and Japanese women must be quite incompetent compared to those of the Scandinavian countries. Or is it that American men are simply much more competent than their Scandinavian counterparts? There is no evidence to support such conclusions. Perhaps one might recognize instead that men and women are channeled by role socialization into (or out of) political avenues of participation.

The point remains that many people talk about democracy, even when women are, by law or convention, not represented fully. Against this background, it is sobering to realize that "women [in Central and Eastern Europe] were very active in the reform movements before the change, but they are almost absent from the political leadership after the change" (Dahlerup, 1991: 3). Of course, the brief tenure of Hanna Suchocka as Prime Minister of Poland stands as something of an exception to this rule. Somewhat parallel, if not isomorphic, arguments can be made on the question of racial and ethnic minority representation, especially in the United States (Duster, 1991). Hence, the degree of gender and related forms of inequality--on the political level as well as other institutional levels--divides the old democracies and confronts new aspirants with a fundamental choice. Perhaps in presenting such choices, the older democracies may question the extent to which the failure to empower diversity contradicts fundamental conceptions of equality. In this way, the unfinished and necessarily dialectic project of democracy may continue, even in older democracies.

A final dimension of debate is less concerned with the formal or informal apparatus of civil society but instead addresses the origin of information and knowledge that makes enlightened public discourse possible. In the nations of the former East bloc, access to the media was heavily controlled. About the only advantage that comes to mind with such an arrangement is that everybody knew that political candor and a critical view were not to be expected. However, the Western-style media present their own structural and cultural challenges to democracy. These forces are not autonomous but linked. For example, to find ethnocentric content in culture, and therefore in the media, is not difficult. But even when the media, through entertainment and programming, simply play to a particular audience, there is still danger if powerful global actors control programming and broadcast it on a world scale. On this point, U.S. producers are responsible for some 79 percent of global film and television exports (Schiller, cited in Perdue, 1993b: 165), and the penetration of CNN and MTV as well as other European programming into Eastern Europe, and Poland specifically, raises questions of cultural hegemony. National programming is underfunded and will have difficulty in competing with the glitter and dash of media giants.

With the wave of American-style privatization sweeping Western Europe, it might be well to offer another warning. "In 1981, there were 46 corporations that controlled most of the business in daily newspapers, magazines, television, books and motion pictures. Five years later the number had shrunk to 29" (Bagdikian, cited in Perdue, 1993b: 174). Heavily dependent on corporation advertising revenue, the media become a vehicle to sell products and ideology to an audience. Bagdikian's point is that centralized control of information flows, whether by the state or immense private corporations, is not compatible with authentic democracy. To oppose successfully such concentration, and to ensure cultural autonomy and media commitment to rational discourse, free inquiry, and cultural enrichment, is a part of the challenge facing would-be democracies--old and new.

The problems of people's rule and the role to be played by the organizations of civil society are complex. In the case of Poland, the crisis is not confined to one or another institution, party, or cause--it is systemic. Wladyslaw Adamski (1991) has argued that the alliance between workers and intellectuals weakened with the assumption of power by Solidarity. Indeed, I have argued elsewhere that a general disintegration was inevitable. The leadership broke with its roots in attempting to resolve as rapidly as possible the barriers to capitalist transformation. Adamski holds that the Polish workers were those who accomplished the Polish revolution and should not now be abandoned as a force for democracy. If they are allowed to remain marginalized and increasingly pauperized, opposition or boycott of the larger institutional sphere of restructuring is inevitable.

The dilemma of "expendable workers" can be joined with a wider view of the challenge to democracy building. Johan Galtung has noted that professing democratic structures and values has not insulated powerful nations from "major forms of international violence such as slavery and colonialism. ....Very much of this done after such milestones on the road toward democracy as 1688, 1776 and 1789 had been passed" (1991: 2). The same can be said of warfare, force, and the threat of force. There is a correlation, of course, between such dubious "democratic" methods of state power and position in a world pyramid of production.

Once arrived at the top of the world there were two obvious problems: not to fall down again, and not to permit too many others [to rise]. The second concern led to a relatively peaked pyramid with few countries on the top and many in the middle and at the bottom. And the first concern led to a number of mechanisms to keep cultural, economic, political and military control on the top: through "division of labor" between senders and receivers of [religious and scientific] truth; between *le cuit and le cru* in the economic sense of processed versus raw goods and services; between decision-makers and those whom the decisions affect; and between those who possess the ultimate means of violence and those who do not. The democracies always went for the best. (Galtung, 1991: 6)

It goes without saying that relational systems (other than market or representational ones) seeking to integrate state, economy, and society have not necessarily been pacifist and egalitarian, either. (With due recognition of Viking plunder aside, Galtung's Norway has done more to renounce bellicose nationalism in the name of democracy than many nation-states.) However, his point is well taken. Democracy and misery, on a world or national scale, too easily coexist, raising questions about the authenticity of people's rule. The dilemma posed in Prague by M. Federico Mayor, Director General of UNESCO, can be translated into English here. "Democracy cannot be reduced to an assortment of institutional rules. It can only live and survive if it is carried by a living experience, an authentic consent, a responsibility which is not directed by a simple count of profits and losses" (1991: 3). So it is that the project of authentic democracy is threatened by rampant inequality, a somber dimension of the paradox of change driving the New Poland toward the dawn of the Twenty-First Century.

CONCLUSION

As this book goes to press in the summer of 1995, conditions remain essentially unchanged in Poland. A sponsored section in the *International Herald Tribune* (June 24-25, 1995) declared that the Polish State had chosen to stay the course of privatization associated with the Balcerowitz plan of 1990. Touting the upsurge in exports and the implementation of National Investment Funds (Perdue, 1995), the more or less unchanged official line is that Poland is preparing for take-off. However, as acknowledged in the Tribune section, the rate of unemployment remained at a staggering 15.3 percent. While GDP had increased in the near-term, this improvement was being constructed from the floor of a deep economic well; a well of massive debt load, labor force downsizing and deindustrialization.

At mid-decade, one exception to the Central and Eastern European crisis (at least in the short-term) appears to be the Czech Republic. Avoiding radical layoffs in state industry, the Czechs registered an unemployment rate of 3.2 percent, while refusing to increase its debt load to burdensome levels. The national government's cumulative load was a nominal 15.7 percent of GDP in 1995 (*International Herald Tribune*, 1995, June 26: 16). However, the case for Czech exceptionalism must be examined closely. To begin, part of the Czech "advantage" comes from its 1993 separation from the Slovak Republic--a movement that had the effect of jettisoning a weaker economic "partner." Moreover, as is evident in World Bank data, GNP per capita declined precipitously from $3,140 U.S. for Czechoslovakia in 1990 to $2,450 U.S. for the Czech Republic in 1992 (World Bank, 1993: 219 and 1994: 163 respectively). In the same years, Polish GNP per capita amounted to $1,690 and $1,910 respectively. It is certainly arguable that the Czech transformation has brought less social pain than in Poland. However, a new paradigm for development will emerge for the region only when the lead economies and organizations of the international community face their common obligations. (See Perdue, 1995, Chapter 14.)

Bibliography

Adamski, W. 1991. "On Strategies and Actions of Transition to Democracy and a Market Economy." Draft paper presented at the International Forum on Culture and Democracy in Prague. Paris: UNESCO.

"Agreements of the Round Table." 1989. Warsaw: Rada Krajowa PRON.

Albert, A. 1986. *The Latest History of Poland. Part 3.* Warsaw: UW.

Andrews, Nicholas G. 1985. *Poland 1980-81: Solidarity Versus the Party.* Washington, DC: National Defense University Press.

Andrzejewski, J. 1986. *Gomulka and Others.* Documents from Central Committee's Archives, 1948-1982. Warsaw: Polska Rzeczpospolita Ludowa.

Aquaviva, S. S. 1979. *The Decline of the Sacred in Industrial Society.* Oxford: B. Blackwell.

Archer, M. 1984. *Social Origins of Educational Systems.* London: Sage.

Ash, Timothy Garton. 1983. *The Polish Revolution: Solidarity 1980-1982.* London: Jonathan Cape.

_____. 1991a. Review of *The Roots of Solidarity: A Political Sociology of Poland's Working Class Democratization* by Roman Laba. The New York Times Review of Books, June 13, vol. 38: 48-51.

_____. 1991b. Review of *The Year 1989: Bronislaw Geremek Relates, Jacek Zakowski Asks* by Bronislaw Geremek and Jacek Zakowski. The New York Times Review of Books, June 13, vol. 38: 46-7.

Baczynski, Jerzy. 1992. "Zrobcie Cos!" (Make Something!) *Polityka* 18, no. 1.

Bartkowski, J. 1990. "Vertical and Horizontal Connections of Local Authorities." In Bartkowski, J., A. Kowalezyk and P. Swianiewicz (eds.), *Strategie Wladz Lokalnych.* Warsaw: UW.

_____. 1991. *Local Activists' Careers.* Warsaw: ISUW.

Berger, Peter L. 1986. *The Capitalist Revolution: Fifty Propositions About Prosperity, Equality and Liberty.* New York: Basic Books.

Berger, Peter and Michael Hsiao. 1991. *The Calculus of Hope: Capitalism*

   and Equality in the Third World. Lanham, MD: University Press of
   America.

Bialer, Seweryn. 1981. "Poland and the Soviet Imperium." *Foreign Affairs*,
   no. 3: 522-539.

Blackledge, D. and B. Hunt. 1985. *Sociological Interpretations of Education.*
   Dover, NH: Croom Helm.

Blazyca, G. 1981. "COMECON and the Polish Crisis." *World Today* 37
   (October): 375-379.

Blejer, Mario I., and Alan Gelb. 1992. "Persistent Economic Decline in
   Central and Eastern Europe." *Transition.* vol. 3, no. 7: 1-3.

Boni, Michael. 1992a. "Pobudzic Aktywnosc." Ministry of Labour and Social
   Policy, *Rynek Pracy* no. 8 (August): 8.

_____. 1992b. "Assumptions of Labor Market Policy." Paper presented at
   Conference on Unemployment: A Challenge for Polish Economy in
   Warsaw, November 26-27. Copied materials.

Boniecki, A. 1983. *The Life of Karol Wojtyla.* Krakow: MIC Znak.

Bousquet, M. M. 1986. "C'est Qui Fait Jouer, C'est Qui Fait Apprendre."
   Perspectives, vol. 4. Paris: UNESCO.

Bromke, Adam. 1987. *The Meaning and Uses of Polish History.* New York:
   Columbia University Press.

Broner, Adam. 1976. "The Degree of Autarky in Centrally Planned
   Economies." *Kylos,* vol. 29: 478-494.

Bruce, L. 1990. "Europe's Locomotive." *Foreign Policy* 78, (Spring): 68-90.

Brumberg, Abraham. 1983. *Poland: Genesis of a Revolution.* New York:
   Random House.

"The Business Outlook In Poland." 1992. *Business Eastern Europe* (August
   31):428.

Buszko, Jozef. 1985. *Historia Polski 1864-1948.* Warsaw: PWN, 417.

Chelminski, Dariusz, Artur Czynczyk and Henryk Sterniczuk. 1991. "New
   Forms of State Ownership in the Process of Privatization in Poland:
   The Case of Commercialization." Paper presented at Conference on
   Privatization, Property and Economic Transformation in the New
   Democracies. Amsterdam, (June 26-29).

Collins, R. 1979. *The Credential Society.* New York: Academic Press.

"Common Encyclopedia." vol. 1-4. 1975. Warsaw: PWN.

Correspondent in Warsaw (unknown). 1993. "Try Again, Poland." *The
   Economist.* 326 (March 27): 53-54.

Council of Europe. 1985. "The Role of Social Security in a Period of
   Economic Difficulties in Countries with Mainly Universal Schemes."
   Third Conference of European Ministers Responsible for Social
   Security, Athens (October 9-11). Strasbourg: 2.

Cox, H. 1965. *The Secular City.* London: SCM Press.

Czaplinski, W. 1966. *On Seventeenth Century Poland.* Warsaw: UW.

Czarnowski, Stefan. 1956. "Redundant People in the Service of Violence."
   Work, vol. 2. Warsaw: 186-193.

Czezowski, T. 1946. *About a University and University Studies.* Torun:
   Ksiegarnia Naukowa.

Dabrowski, Janusz, Michal Federowitz, and Anthony Levitas. 1991. *State Owned Enterprises in 1990*. Unpublished mimeograph. Krakow: Jagiellonian University Institute of Sociology.

Dahlerup, Drude, 1991. "Unfinished Democracy." Draft of a paper presented at the International Forum on Culture and Democracy in Prague. Paris: UNESCO.

Darnton, John. 1993. "Enormous Changes at the Last Minute." *The New York Times* (June 13): 24.

Davis, Norman. 1981. *God's Playground: A History of Poland. Vol. I: The Origins to 1775*. New York: Columbia University Press.

_____. 1982. *God's Playground: A History of Poland. Vol. II: 1795 to the Present*. Oxford, England: Oxford University Press.

"Demand Outpacing Supply." 1992. *The Warsaw Voice* (September 6).

De Michelis, G. 1990. "Reaching Out to the East." *Foreign Policy* 79, (Summer): 44-55.

De Soto, Hernando. 1989. *The Other Path*. New York: Harper and Row.

Dickson, David. 1987. "Council of Europe Study: 'European' Cooperation is West European." *Science* (September 4): 11-14.

Donahue, John D. 1989. *The Privatization Decision: Public Ends, Private Means*. New York: Basic Books.

Dryll, I. 1991. "Unemployment - Fiction or Dilemma?" *Zycie Gospodarcze*. no. 5.

Dunin-Wasowicz, Maria. 1991. *Local Leaders and the Management of Local Development in Poland*. Paris: Organisation for Economic Co-operation and Development.

Durkheim, E. 1956. *Sociology and Society*. New York: Free Press.

Duster, Troy. 1991. "A New and Emerging Corruption of Ethnic Diversity." Draft paper presented at the International Forum on Culture and Democracy in Prague. Paris: UNESCO.

Etzioni, A. 1990. "Poland: The Big Leap Just Might Flop." *International Herald Tribune* (June 26): 4.

"European Community Charter of Fundamental Social Rights: Charting a New Course." 1990. (January): 45-46 *Geographic Magazine* 62.

"The Fading of Red." 1994. *The Economist* 330, no. 7846 (January 15): 56.

Fields, Gary. 1991. "The Road From Gdansk: How Solidarity Found Haven in the Marketplace." *Monthly Review* (July-August): 95-121.

Foner, Phillip and Brewster Chamberlain. 1977. *Friedrich A. Sorge's Labor Movement in the United States*. Westport, CT: Greenwood Press.

Foucault, M. 1979. *Discipline and Punish: The Birth of the Prison*, translated by A. Sheridan. New York: Vantage.

French, Hilary F. 1990. Green Revolutions: Environmental Reconstruction in Eastern Europe and the Soviet Union. Washington, DC: The World Watch Institute.

_____. 1994. "Rebuilding the World Bank." In Lester R. Brown et al., (eds.), *State of the World*, 156-176. New York: W. W. Norton.

Fukuyama, Francis. 1992. *The End of History and the Last Man*. New York: The Free Press.

Galtung, Johan. 1991. "Why are Democracies so Belligerent?" Draft paper presented at International Forum on Culture and Democracy in Prague. Paris: UNESCO.

George, Susan. 1990. *A Fate Worse Than Debt*. New York: Grove.

Geremek, Bronislaw. 1991. *Rok 1989: Bronislaw Geremek Odpowiada, Jacek Zakowski Pyta*. Warsaw: Plejada.

Germani, Gino. 1981. *The Sociology of Modernization*. New Brunswick: Transaction.

Gierowski, J. 1991. "Personal Balance." *Krakow*. no. 3.

Gockowski, J. 1991. "Theses About a University." *Teksty* no. 2.

_____. 1991. "A University - A Guardian and Spokesman of Scholarly Ethos." In J. Gockowski and K. Pigon (eds.), *Professional Ethics of Scholars*. Wroclaw-Warsaw-Krakow: Zaklad Narodowy im Ossolinskich, Wydawnictwo Polskiej Akademii Nauk, 17.

Goodwyn, Lawrence. 1991. *Breaking the Barrier: The Rise of Solidarity in Poland*. New York: Oxford University Press.

Gora, Marek, Irena Kotowska, Tomasz Panek, and Jaroslaw Podgorski. 1991. "Labour Market, Industrial Relations and Social Policy: A Report on Poland." Paris: Organisation for Economic Co-operation and Development - International Labour Office.

Gordon, Z. D. 1981. "Enseignants Efficases; Enseigner et Etre Soi-meme." Quebec: Unpublished draft.

Gramsci, Antonio. 1971. *Selections from the Prison Notebooks*. London: New Left Books.

Grell, J. 1989. "Formation of Power Elites in the People's Poland and Political Culture." Poznan: UP.

Grodecki, R. 1969. "History of Jews in Poland Till the End of the 14th Century." In J. Wyrozumski (ed.), *Poland of the Piast Dynasty*. Warsaw: UW.

Grunewald, Bjorn. 1991. "Joint Ventures and East-West Cooperation: A Case From Poland." Stockholm: Swedish Employers' Confederation.

Grzybowski, K. 1990. "The Council for Mutual Economic Assistance and the European Community." *American Journal of International Law* 84 (January): 284-292.

Gusfield, Joseph (ed.) 1970. *Protest, Reform and Revolt: A Reader in Social Movements*. New York: John Wiley and Sons.

Habermas, Jurgen. 1976. *Legitimation Crisis*. London: Heinemann.

_____. 1987. *The Theory of Communicative Action*. vols. 1 and 2. Cambridge, England: Polity Press.

Halicz, Emanuel. 1982. *Polish National Liberation Struggles and the Genesis of the Modern Nation: Collected Papers of Emanuel Halicz*. Translated from Polish by Roger A. Clarke. Odense, Denmark: Odense University Press.

Hanks, Steve H. and Alan Walters. 1993. "The High Cost of Jeffrey Sachs." *Forbes* 151. no. 13 (June 21): 52.

Hayek, Friedrich A. 1960 *Constitution of Liberty*. London: Routledge & Kegan Paul.

Heberle, Rudolph. 1951. *Social Movements: An Introduction to Political Sociology.* New York: Appleton-Century-Croft.

Hirschman, Albert. 1970. *Exit, Voice and Loyalty: Responses to Decline in Firms, Organizations and States.* Cambridge, MA: Harvard University Press.

_____. 1977. *Passions and Interests: Political Arguments for Capitalism Before its Triumph.* Princeton: Princeton University Press.

Huntington, Samuel. 1984. "Will More Countries Become Democratic?" *Political Science Quarterly* 99: 193-218.

Jagiello, E. M. 1992. In "*Polish Foreign Trade in 1991.*" Warsaw: Foreign Trade Research Institute.

Jasinska-Kania, Aleksandra. 1983. "Rationalization and Legitimation Crisis: The Relevance of Marxian and Weberian Works for an Explanation of the Political Order's Legitimacy Crisis in Poland." *The Journal of the British Sociological Association,* vol. 17, no. 2 (May): 157-164.

Jaspers, K. 1978. "Research, Work, Education, Teaching." *Znak,* no. 6: 733.

John Paul II. 1979. "Social Teachings," vol. 1. *Pilgrimage to Poland.* Krakow: Krakow Diocese (June 2-10).

_____. 1983. "Second Visit to Poland of John Paul II." *L'Osservatore Romano.* Special Edition (June 16-23).

_____. 1987. "The Third Visit of John Paul II." *L'Osservatore Romano.* Special Edition (June 8-14).

Kabaj, Mieczyslaw. 1992. "Elements of Program Counteracting Unemployment." *Social Policy,* no. 1.

Kaminski, A. 1991. "Reformability and the Development Potential of Socio-economic Orders: The Case of Communism." In W. Kozek and W. Morawski (eds.) *Society Facing Challenges of the Market Economy.* Warsaw: UW.

Kawalec, W. 1974. "Polish Ministry of Labour, Wages and Social Affairs: A New Instrument for Social Policy." *International Labour Review* 110 (August): 145-163.

Kelly, Tim. 1991. "Telecommunications and the Transition to a Market-Based Economy." Paris: Organisation for Economic Co-operation and Development.

Kemp-Welch, A. 1983. *The Birth of Solidarity: The Gdansk Negotiations, 1980.* Translated and introduced by A. Kemp-Welch. London: Maxmillan in association with St. Antony's College, Oxford.

Kennedy, Michael D. 1991. *Professionals, Power, and Solidarity in Poland: A Critical Sociology of Soviet-type Society.* Cambridge, England; New York: Cambridge University Press.

Kersten, K. 1990. "The Birth of the Power System: Poland 1943-1948." Poznan: SAWW.

Kimbell, Lucy. 1993. "Not Much Solidarity in Solidarnosc Now." *New Statesman & Society* 6 (June 18): 18-19.

Klich, Jacek. 1992. "The Changes in the Polish Economy and Social Policy in the beginning of 1990's." *Yearbook of Polish Labour Law and Social Policy*, vol. 2. Krakow: Jagiellonian University Press.

Klich, Jacek and Krystyna Poznanska. (forthcoming). "Some Active Measures to Countervail Unemployment in Poland: A Regional Analysis." *Yearbook of Polish Labour Law and Social Policy*. Krakow: Jagiellonian University Press.

Kogela, Krzysztof. 1988. "Speciality of the Enterprise: Protection." In W. Morawski and W. Kozek (eds.), *Breakdown of the Statist Order*. Warsaw: UW.

Koj, A. 1991. "A Careful Optimism." *Krakow*, no. 3: 5.

"Koncepcja Programu Ksztalcenia Ogolnego w Polskich Szkolach." 1991. Warsaw: Ministry of National Education.

Kornai, Janos. 1990. *The Road to a Free Economy*. New York: W. W. Norton.

Laba, Roman. 1991. *The Roots of Solidarity: A Political Sociology of Poland's Working Class Democratization*. Princeton, NJ: Princeton University Press.

Larembka, Paul. 1993. "Poland: The Deepening Crisis in the Summer of 1992." *Monthly Review* 44 (January): 21-29.

Laurent, Pierre-Henri. 1994. "Widening Europe: The Dilemmas of Community Success." *The Annals* (January): 124-140.

Le Bras, G. 1966. "Vitality of the Church in France." In *People-Faith-Church: Sociological Analyses*. Warsaw: UW.

Lecler, J. 1964. *History of Tolerance in the Reformation Age*. Warsaw: UW.

Leven, Bozena. 1993. "Short-term Effects of Economic Transition on Inequality and Poverty: The Polish Case." *Journal of Economic Issues* 27 (March): 237-243.

Levin, I. 1942-1943. "The Protection of Jewish Religious Rights by Royal Edicts in Ancient Poland." *Bulletin of the Polish Institute of Arts and Sciences in America I*: 556-7.

Lipton, David and Jeffrey Sachs. 1991. "Privatization in Eastern Europe: The Case of Poland." In Vittorio Corbo, Fabrizio Coricelli, Jan Bossak (eds.), *Reforming Eastern and Central European Economies: Initial Results and Challenges, a World Bank Symposium*. Washington, DC: The World Bank.

Lovenduski J., and Woodall J. 1987. *Politics and Society in Eastern Europe*. Bloomington: Indiana University Press.

Ludlow, Howard T. 1975. "The Role of Trade Unions in Poland." *Political Science Quarterly* 90, no. 2: 315-324.

Mannheim. 1968. *Ideology and Utopia: An Introduction to the Sociology of Knowledge*. Translated by Louis Wirth and Edward Shils. New York: Harcourt, Brace and World (originally published in 1936).

Markovic, Mihailo. 1991. "Political Culture and Democracy." Prepared for the International Forum on Democracy and Culture in Prague. Paris: UNESCO.

Mason, David S. 1989. "Solidarity as a New Social Movement." *Political Science Quarterly*, 104, no. 1: 41-58.

Mayor, M. Federico. 1991. "Discourse." Draft paper presented at the International Forum for Culture and Democracy in Prague. Paris: UNESCO.

McClelland, David C. 1961. *The Achieving Society.* New York: The Free Press.

Micewski, A. 1978. *Rule Together or Not Lie.* Paris: Unpublished manuscript.

Michnik, Adam. 1990. "Two Faces of Eastern Europe." *The New Republic* (November 12).

Miklaszewska, Ewa. 1992. "Problems With Attracting Foreign Capital to Poland." *Economics Papers* no. 6 (forthcoming). Krakow: Jagiellonian University Press.

Mikulowski-Pomorski, J. 1991. "Collectivation in Relation to Differentiation of the World of Science." In J. Gockowski and K. Pigon (eds.), *Professional Ethics of Scholars.* Wroclaw-Warsaw-Krakow: Zaklad Narodowy im Ossolinskich, Wydawnictwo Polskiej Akademii Nauk.

Morawska, Ewa. 1992. "On Comparative and Historical Sociology." Newsletter of the ASA Section on Comparative and Historical Sociology (Spring): 2-4.

Mujzel, Jan. 1991. "The Problems of Post-Communism Transformation, Recession and Privatization." Warsaw: Polish Academy of Sciences, Institute of Economics.

Nadle, Marlene. 1990. "Second Thoughts on Solidarity (A Polish Opinion)." *The Progressive* 54 (January: 24).

Narojek, W. 1991. *The Socialist Welfare State.* Warsaw: UW.

Oberschall, Anthony. 1973. *Social Conflict and Social Movements.* Englewood Cliffs, NJ: Prentice-Hall.

Oden, Michael. 1993. "National and Local Decision-making in the Design, Implementation and Financing of Vocational and Technical Education." *Education and the Economy in Central Europe.* Paris: OECD, (October): 9-30.

Offe, Claus. 1991. "Statement for International Forum on Democracy and Culture in Prague." Paris: UNESCO.

Organisation for Economic Co-operation and Development. 1991a. "Labour Markets in Central and Eastern Europe: Recent Developments." Unpublished draft. Paris: OECD.

_____. 1991b. "Memorandum of Understanding Between the OECD and the Government of the Republic of Poland concerning the Programme: Partners in Transition." Paris: OECD.

_____. 1991c. "Partnership in Transition-Poland: 1991/92 Programme." Restricted rough draft. Paris: OECD.

_____. 1992a. Conference on Education and the Economy in Central and Eastern Europe, "Financing Education and Training in Central and Eastern Europe: A New Social Contract." (June 29-July 1). Paris: OECD.

_____. 1992b. Conference on Education and the Economy in Central and Eastern Europe. "Report on Educational Training in Poland During the Transformation of the Socio-Economic System." Paris: OECD.

Ortega y Gasset, J. 1978. "University Mission." *Znak* no. 6: 720-721.

Parkin, Frank. 1972. *Class Inequality and the Political Order: Social Stratification in Capitalist and Communist Societies.* London: Grenada.

Pelczar, A. 1991. "Community of Masters and Pupils." *Krakow.* no. 3: 3.

Perdue, William D. 1986. *Sociological Theory: Explanation, Paradigm and Ideology.* Palo Alto, CA: Mayfield Publishers.

_____. 1993a. "The Coming Legitimation Crisis of the United Nations." *Nord Sud XXI* 4: 67-107.

_____. 1993b. *Systemic Crisis: Global Issues and Social Problems.* Fort Worth, TX: Harcourt Brace Jovanovich.

_____. 1995. *Modernization Crisis: The Transformation of Poland.* Westport, CT: Praeger.

Perlez, Jane. 1993a. "Polish Ex-Communists Resurgent: Voters Show Anger on Economy." *The New York Times* 143 (September 20): A1.

_____. 1993b. "Why Poland Swung to Left." *The New York Times* 143 (September 21): A4.

Pond, Elizabeth. 1993. "Poland's Competitive Edge." *Europe: Magazine of the European Community* (November), no. 331: 22-24.

Poznanski, Kazimierz Z. 1992. "Privatization of the Polish Economy: Problems of Transition." *Soviet Studies,* 44, no. 4.

_____. 1993. "Restructuring of Property Rights in Poland: A Study in Evolutionary Economics" *East European Politics and Societies* 7 (no. 3): 395-419.

Project Liberty: Harvard University and The Adansic Institute for Market Economics. 1991. *The Social and Political Consequences of Decentralization and Privatization.* Cambridge, MA: JFK School of Government.

"Projekt Karty Praw i Wolnosci." 1990. Elaborated by the Helsinki Committee (of Human Rights) in Poland. *Rzeczpospolita* (November).

Rosenberg, Tina. 1993. "Meet the New Boss, Same as the Old Boss." *Harpers Magazine* 286 (May): 47-53.

Rostow, W. W. 1964. "The Takeoff Into Self-sustained Growth." In Amitai Etzioni and Eva Etzioni (eds.), *Social Change,* 285-300. New York: Basic Books.

Rude, George. 1980. *Ideology and Popular Protest.* New York: Pantheon.

Scott, Alan. 1990. *Ideology and the New Social Movements.* London: Unwin Hyman.

Short Philosophical Dictionary. 1955. Warsaw: UW.

Sinclairem, P. 1991. "There Will be Time for Shakespeare." Interview given to journalist of *Economic Life,* no. 1.

Singer, Daniel. 1989a. "Solidarity's Victory: Partnership for Poland?" *The Nation* 248 (June 26): 878-881.

_____. 1989b. "Solidarity: The Road to Power (Poland)." *The Nation* 249 (October 9): 376.

_____. 1990. "Solidarity Lost." *The Nation* 251 (December 17): 756-757.

Skolnick, Jerome and Elliot Currie. 1991. *Crisis in American Institutions.* New York: HarperCollins.

So, Alvin Y. 1990. *Social Change and Development: Modernization, Dependency, and World-System Theories.* Newbury Park, London; New Delhi: Sage Publications.

Sobczyk, Arkadiusz. 1992a."Unemployment in Poland - Basic Characteristics." *Yearbook of Polish Labour Law and Social Policy,* vol. 3, Krakow: Jagiellonian University Press.

_____. 1992b. "Unemployment Schemes in Poland and Hungary - A Comparative Analysis." *Yearbook of Polish Labour Law and Social Policy,* vol. 3, Krakow: Jagiellonian University Press.

_____. (forthcoming). "Privatization in Poland - Economic and Legal Approaches."*Economic Papers,* no.5, Krakow: Jagiellonian University Press.

Stark, David. 1992a. "Can Designer Capitalism Work in Central and Eastern Europe?" *Transition,* 3, no. 5.

_____. 1992b. "From System Identity to Organizational Diversity: Analyzing Social Change in Eastern Europe." *Contemporary Sociology.* 21, no. 30: 229-304.

"Statistical Information." 1992. *Unemployment in Poland, I-II Quarter. 1991.* (July). Warsaw: Central Statistical Office.

Strzelecki, J. 1989. "A Lyrical Model of Socialism." Warsaw: Czytelnik.

Suchodolski, B. 1974. "Who is a Man?" *Wiedza Powszechna.* Warsaw: UW.

Swiatkowski, Andrzej. 1991. "Workers and Union Representation at the Enterprise Level in Poland." *Yearbook of Polish Labour Law and Social Policy ,* 63. vol. 2, Krakow: Jagiellonian University Press.

Szkolny, Michael. 1981. "Revolution in Poland." *Monthly Review.* vol. 33, no. 2 (June).

Szopa, Andrzej. 1987. "Economic Mechanisms of Fixed Assets Reproduction in Socialist Economy." Krakow: Krakow Academy of Economics.

Sztompka, Piotr. 1991. "The Intangibles and Imponderables of the Transition to Democracy." *Studies in Comparative Communism.* XXIV, no. 3: 295-311.

_____. 1993. *The Sociology of Social Change.* Oxford: Blackwell.

Tilly, Charles. 1984. *Big Structures, Large Processes, Huge Comparisons.* New York: Russell Sage.

Tischner, Jozef. 1984. *The Spirit of Solidarity.* Translated by Marek B. Zaleski and Benjamin Fiora. San Francisco, CA: Harper & Row.

Touraine, A. 1981. *The Voice and the Eye: An Analysis of Social Movements.* Cambridge, England: Cambridge University Press.

_____. 1991. "Qu'est-ce que la Democratie Aujourd'hui? (Version Provisoire)." Prepared for the International Forum on Democracy and Culture in Prague. Paris: UNESCO.

Touraine, A., F. Dubet, M. Wieviorka, and J. Strzeleck. 1983. *Solidarity: The Analysis of a Social Movement: Poland, 1980-81.* In collaboration with Grazyna Gesicka, et al. Translated by David Denby. Cambridge, New York: Cambridge University Press.
United Nations Development Programme. 1992. *Human Development Report, 1992.* New York: Oxford University Press.
United States Bureau of Census. 1990. *Statistical Abstract of the United States.* Washington, DC: U. S. Government Printing Office.
United States Department of State. 1990. *Fact Sheet: Council of Europe.* Dispatch (December 31). Washington, DC: U. S. Government Printing Office.
Vetulani, A. 1962. "The Jews in Medieval Poland." *Jewish Journal of Sociology* IV: 274-294.
Vinton, Louisa. 1993. "Pawlak and Kwasniewski: How Post Communist are They?" Research Report (October 29).
Vuorikeri, Veikko. 1991. "Important Features of Development of New Enterprises." Paper presented at the International Conference on National, Regional and Local Development in Multi-Party Democracies: Will Democracy Succeed? (July 8-10). Paris: OECD.
Walesa, Lech. 1987. *A Path of Hope.* London: Collins Harvill.
_____. 1989. *The Road of Hope.* Krakow: Znak.
The Warsaw Voice. 1992. no. 38 (September 20).
Weber, Max. 1949. *The Methodology of the Social Sciences.* New York: Free Press.
Wedel, Janine R. 1992. *The Unplanned Society: Poland During and After Communism.* Edited, annotated, and with introduction by Janine R. Wedel. New York: Columbia University Press.
Wereszycki, H. 1981. "Political History of Poland: 1864-1918." Krakow: Jagiellonian University Press.
Wilkin, Jerzy. 1989. "Private Agriculture and Socialism." In Roger Clarke (ed.), *Poland: The Economy in the 1980s.* Chicago: St. James Press, 64.
Wilson, Ernest J. III. "The Third Phase of the Polish Revolution: Property Rights." Unpublished paper.
Winiecki, Jan. 1991a. "Post-Soviet-Type Economies in Transition: What Have We Learned From the Polish Transition Programme in its First Year." *Weltwirtschatfliche Archiv.* 126 no. 4: 765-790.
_____. 1991b. "Resistance to Change in the Soviet Economic System: A Property Rights Approach." (unpublished). London.
Wolfe, Alan. 1978. *The Seamy Side of Democracy.* New York: Longman.
Wong, Siu-Lun. 1988. "The Applicability of Asian Family Values to Other Sociocultural Settings." In Peter L. Berger and Hsin-Huang Michael Hsiao (eds.), *In Search of an East Asian Development Model,* 134-154. Brunswick, NJ: Transaction.
Woodall, Jean. 1981. "New Social Factors in the Unrest in Poland." *Government and Opposition* 16 (Winter): 37-57.
World Almanac. 1995. Mahwah, NJ: Funk and Wagnalls.

World Bank. 1990. *An Agricultural Strategy for Poland.* Washington, DC: The World Bank (Polish, European Community Task Force).

————. 1991. *World Development Report, 1991: The Challenge of Development.* New York: Oxford University Press.

————. 1993. *World Development Report, 1993: Investing in Health.* New York: Oxford University Press.

————. 1994. *World Development Report, 1994: Infrastructure for Development.*

Zarembka, Paul. 1993. "Poland: The Deepening Crisis in the Summer of 1992." *Monthly Review* (November): 21-29.

Zarnowski, Janusz. 1973. *Society of the Second Republic.* Warsaw: UW.

Zenczykowski, T. 1983. *Two Committees 1920, 1944: Poland in Lenin's and Stalin's Plans.* Paris: Editions Spotkania.

Zimon, Henry A. 1979. "Regional Inequalities in Poland." *Economic Geography* 55 (July): 242-252.

Znaniecki, F. 1974. *Contemporary People and Civilization of the Future.* Warsaw: PWN, 145-146.

Index

Nomenklatura, 13, 20, 64, 67, 79, 81
Non-Party Bloc, 80
North-South gap, 91
Nowa Huta, 13

Oberschall, Anthony, 35
Offe, Claus, 106
Opium Wars, 90
Order Paradigm, 3. *See also*
    Functionalism
Organisation for Economic Co-
    operation and Development
    (OECD), 89, 94-104
Organisation for European Economic
    Co-operation (OEEC), 94

Pact on State Enterprises, 80
Paris Commune Shipyard
    (Gydnia), 39, 46
Parkin, Frank, 24
Parsons, Talcott, 3, 89
Partners in Transition Pro-
    gramme, 96. *See also*
    Organisation for Economic
    Co-operation and Development
Path of Hope, 39
Patriotic Movement of National
    Salvation (PRON), 72
Pawlak, W., 81, 82
Perestroika, 66
Perry, Matthew, 90
Phenomenology, 89
Pilsudski, Marshal, 11, 13, 62
Pluralism, 4, 50, 86, 89. *See
    also* contractualism
Polish August, 48
Polish Committee of National
    Liberation (PKNW), 12
Polish Peasant Party (PSL), 80, 81,
    82
Polish United Workers Party
    (PZPR), 19
Polityka Polska (Polish Politics),
    69
Pomian, Krzysztof, 20
Popieluszko, Father Jerzy, 61
Postconventional orientation, 49

Post-structuralism, 57
Poznanski, Kazimierz, 66

Rakowski, M., 72
Reagan, Ronald, 73
Realism, 89
"Real socialism," 13, 37, 42,
    61, 62
Reich, Robert, 102
Relational logic, 34-38, 89-
    91
Relativistic logic, 89-90
Robotnik (The Worker), 22,
    56
Rokossowski, Konstantin,
    19
Rostow, Walt, 87, 104
Round Table, 70-73, 85
Rousseau, Jean-Jacques, 60
Rude, G., 37

Sachs, Jeffrey, 76
Scientific management (in
    the People's Poland),
    24-25.
Self-management, 64, 66, 68
Semiotics, 15
"Shock Therapy," 76-83, 92,
    105. *See also* Will to
    strike
Sienkiewicz, Henry, 1
Sit-down strike, 33
Skinheads, 78, 79
Smelser, Neil, 3
Smith, Adam, 88
So, Alvin, 86, 87
Social action, 8-9
Sociological intervention, 8
Sociology of Development,
    89
Solidarnosc (Solidarity), 1,
    85, 107; the ideology of,
    40-50;
    and marketization, 67-73,
    110. *See also* Derivative
    ideology
Srodowisko, 51

Stalin, J., 13, 18, 19
State and Social Revolution, 69
Strzelecki, Jerzy, 69
Suchocka, H., 75, 80, 81, 85
Systemic crisis, 11-18, 23, 27, 37,
    65, 67. *See also* legitimation
    crisis
Szkolny, M., 44

Thatcher, Margaret, 73
Touraine, Alain, 5, 7-9, 27,
    63, 64, 105
Trade: and world market expansion,
    17; Balance of, 15-16, 23-24, 27
Tyminski, S., 74

Unemployment, 77, 100
Uneven development, 25
Unipolarity, 2
United Nations Development
    Programme, 91, 93, 97
United Nations Economic
    Commission, 94
United Nations Educational,
    Scientific and Cultural
    Organization (UNESCO),
    104-111

Values: and modernization, 89

Wajda, Andrzej, 34
Walentynowicz, Anna, 39
Walesa, Lech, 1, 22, 34, 39,
    42, 53, 54, 65, 66, 69, 70,
    71, 72, 73, 75, 80, 85, 107
Walicki, Andrzej, 69
Wallerstein, Immanuel, 88
Warski Shipyard, 33, 39
Weber, Max, 6, 28, 29, 40
Wedel, Janine, 2
Wierzbicki, Piotr, 69
Wilderness Years, 65
Will to strike, 79-80
Wojtyla, Karol, 44. *See also* John
    Paul II
Women in politics, 109
Woodall, Jean, 24

Work Councils, 29, 64
Workers' Council Law of 1956, 19
World Bank, 75, 82, 89, 90, 95, 96
World market absorption, 67-69,
    94-104
World-System Theory, 88
Wyszynski, Cardinal, 44, 60, 61

Zarembka, Paul, 78

About the Author

WILLIAM DAN PERDUE is Professor of Sociology and Director of Contemporary World Studies at Eastern Washington University. His books include *The Ideology of Social Problems* (1981) (with Charles Reasons); *Sociological Theory: Explanation, Paradigm and Ideology* (1986); *Terrorism and the State: A Critique of Domination Through Fear* (1989); *Systemic Crisis: Problems in Society, Politics and World Order* (1993) and *Modernization Crisis: The Transformation of Poland* (1995) (with T. Borkowski, S. Palka and A. Szopa). He is a frequent contributor to the international literature on conflict resolution, United Nations reform, social change and development. A recipient of his university's Trustee's Medal, he is currently at work on the *Fourth Paradigm: Social Change and Development in the New Africa.*

ISBN 0-275-95295-9

HARDCOVER BAR CODE